ABINGDON PILLARS
OF THEOLOGY

AUGUSTINE

EUGENE TESELLE

Abingdon Press
Nashville

AUGUSTINE

This book is printed on acid-free paper.

Library of Congress Cataloging-in-Publication Data

TeSelle, Eugene, 1931-
  Augustine / Eugene TeSelle.
    p. cm.—(Abingdon pillars of theology)
  Includes bibliographical references and indexes.
  ISBN 0-687-05361-7 (binding: paper 6 x 9 : alk. paper)
  1. Augustine, Saint, Bishop of Hippo. I. Title. II. Series.

  BR65.A9T39 2006
  230'.14'092—dc22

                                                                2005016171

06 07 08 09 10 11 12 13 14 15—10 9 8 7 6 5 4 3 2 1
MANUFACTURED IN THE UNITED STATES OF AMERICA

CONTENTS

PREFACE

This book comes out of thirty-five years of seminars on Augustine, moving forward, backward, and sideways through his writings, profiting from the questions and insights of many students. It also comes out of participation in the work of a host of scholars who find Augustine's thought fascinating because of its richness and complexity. The Selected Bibliography at the end will give some basic leads for further reading.

Much of what is said here was developed for a course sponsored by Retirement in Learning at Vanderbilt University in the spring of 2004. It made me "get to the point" about a number of topics; it was even more helpful to hear the reactions of other senior citizens who continue to stay alert to intellectual and social issues.

Parts of chapters 4 and 5 were developed in a Cole Lecture at Vanderbilt Divinity School at my retirement in 1999. In writing several chapters, I have condensed, revised, or augmented passages in several of my own recent publications. In chapters 1 and 8, I have drawn upon *Living in Two Cities: Augustinian Trajectories in Political Thought* (Scranton: University of Scranton Press, 1998). A few pages draw upon "Justice, Love, Peace," in *Augustine Today* (ed. Richard John Neuhaus; Grand Rapids: Eerdmans, 1993), 88-110. Several paragraphs have been adapted from "Pelagius, Pelagianism" in *Augustine Through the Ages: An Encyclopedia* (ed. Allen D. Fitzgerald, O.S.A.; Grand Rapids: Eerdmans, 1999), pp. 633-40. In chapter 5 I have drawn upon several pages in "Exploring the Inner Conflict: Augustine's Sermons on Romans 7 and 8," in Frederick Van Fleteren and Joseph C. Schnaubelt, *Augustine: Biblical Exegete* (vol. 5 of Collectanea Augustiniana; ed. Joseph C. Schnaubelt and Frederick Van Fleteren; New York: Peter Lang, 2000), 333-65. All scripture translations are my own; in some cases they reflect the readings in the Old Latin version used by Augustine.

CHRONOLOGY

INTRODUCTION

Call him Au*gus'*tine, or *Aug'*ustine. It probably depends where you, or your teachers, went to school. Those who prefer Au*gus'*tine often use Au*gus'*tine for the city in Florida or for the first missionary from Rome to the Anglo-Saxons, Augustine of Canterbury. The old English contraction was *Austin*, as in *S'n't Austin* or *Austin Friars*.

He was born in North Africa (in what is now eastern Algeria) in Thagaste, sixty miles south of Hippo on the Mediterranean, where he would later be bishop. Although he lived on the continent of Africa, he was not a black sub-Saharan African. The genetic makeup in this territory was first Berber, then Punic or Phoenician (colonizers from the eastern Mediterranean with a language close to Hebrew), and then Roman. They knew about black sub-Saharan Africans, but contacts were through trade, not migration.

When Augustine was born in 354, the Roman Empire included all the territories surrounding the Mediterranean; it reached as far east as Mesopotamia and as far north as the Danube, the Rhine, and Britain, up to Hadrian's Wall. Christianity had been introduced into Ethiopia to the south and Armenia and Georgia on the east side of the Black Sea, all of them independent kingdoms. Constantine and his sons gave Christianity a favored role, although they tolerated the older religious traditions.

During Augustine's lifetime the frontiers of the Empire were weakened. The Goths crossed the Danube, established themselves in what is now Romania, and then wandered farther west; the Vandals crossed the Rhine and moved into Spain. The Roman legions were withdrawn from Britain in 407 to protect the continent of Europe. Vandal invaders crossed into Africa during Augustine's last years, ending Roman rule in the areas that we now call Algeria and Tunisia. It was a time of rapid change.

Augustine's own life went through several major changes. And his thought was constantly evolving as he dealt simultaneously with a number of questions (a French scholar has characterized it as "cinematic"). Many of his works were occasioned by controversies; in them he makes full use of his rhetorical skills, sizing up the issues, making distinctions, and presenting his case. But he is not concerned merely to win arguments. There is a spirit of constant inquiry in his writings, a willingness to reconsider issues in the light of new questions, new information, new perspectives.

It has been said that "the past is a foreign country: they do things differently there."[1] In many ways, Augustine's understanding of the cosmos and of human life is different from ours. Whether different or similar, we must be aware of the nature of all interpretation. It begins with careful examination of past situations, events, and thoughts; then it demands empathy in thinking along with people in the past and translating their questions into our own idiom; and in the end we must deal with these questions in our own day. It may happen that we will answer them in much the same way, making adjustments for differing assumptions about the world and increased knowledge in many areas. Or it may be that differing assumptions and new information will lead us to a very different answer.

Augustine has been influential because of his doctrinal formulations, of course. But an even more important reason is that he is so stimulating, for he engaged in constant inquiry. Often he goes through all the possible answers to a question. Usually the last possibility is the one that seems strongest to him. But he requires the reader to go through the process with him and make the final judgment. He himself often changed his opinion on questions, in small and large ways. Thus *what* he asserted may be less important than *how* and *why* he came to a position. He is a major illustration of John Henry Newman's dictum that "to live is to change, and to be perfect is to have changed often."[2]

We begin with the *Confessions*, where, in telling about his own journey, he finds that he must engage in various kinds of intellectual inquiry. Then we look at major themes in his thought, following a more or less chronological order. We must start with his philosophical interest in Platonism, which set the framework for his thinking about human fulfillment, evil, and creation. These topics then bring us to his somber judgments about the human self, shaped by Paul's emphasis on sin and salvation. Finally, we turn to his concern with broader matters outside the self: the church, its doctrines, the course of human history, and the relation of Christianity to political matters. In all of these ways he has influenced the life and thought of the West. Even those who think he was wrong in his conclusions respect his willingness to confront problems and think through their implications.

CHAPTER ONE

AUGUSTINE'S JOURNEY

Augustine wrote the *Confessions* in 397, soon after becoming a bishop. They are the first full-scale autobiography, much larger than any previous first-person work. He had already invented the title, and the genre, of *Soliloquies*—"conversations with myself." This was one of the works written soon after his religious conversion; they already contain short autobiographical passages that have been called "the first *Confessions*."[1]

In writing the *Confessions*, Augustine was not doing something totally new. There had been others, pagan and Christian, who told about their intellectual and spiritual quests, exhorting others to follow their path to philosophical or religious conversion. The Greco-Roman world was very much like our own: diverse and cosmopolitan, presenting a variety of options as people sought "meaning" in life. But Augustine told his story with much wider scope and in a new way that became a model for later autobiographies—or something to react against. Rousseau's *Confessions*, written in the eighteenth century, intentionally took a new and different direction.

When he wrote the *Confessions*, Augustine was 43, the age of "midlife crisis" with its questioning about one's past and future. It could have been stimulated by a number of factors. He had just written *On Christian Instruction*, where he considered the relationships between Christianity and classical culture; perhaps this got him thinking about his own encounters with both traditions. And then his friend Alypius had been asked by an Italian bishop to tell about the beginnings of the monastic life in Africa; the section on Alypius in Book VI seems to have been written first. The *Confessions* may also have been written in self-defense. Here was a former Manichaean, an intellectual whom many regarded as arrogant, who had been elected bishop in a manner contrary to the canons of the Council of Nicaea (no one in Hippo knew about them). And there may have been negative reactions to his new theory of predestination, put forward about a year before the *Confessions*. If so, he trumped his critics, acknowledging many sins and shortcomings but tracing the hand of God throughout. There are several ways of reading the *Confessions*: as a narrative about his own past; as a gold mine for psychoanalysts (a case can be made for both oedipal and narcissistic themes); as reflection about, and interpretation of, his own past; as clues to influences upon his thinking; and as a literary product with an intriguing stylistic texture.

Augustine is always the intellectual. Passages are never purely factual or expressive. The purpose of recalling his life before God is to engage in constant questioning, trying to interpret events that seemed incoherent or puzzling as bare experience. Passages often reflect his theories—or perplexities—about the soul, its impulses, its origin, and its destiny. Much of their persuasiveness comes from the way they draw in the reader and stimulate similar self-examination. Peppered throughout the text are quotations from the Bible in the Old Latin translation. This looked exotic and inelegant to the cultured, but Augustine heard it as the voice of God, offering the framework within which to orient and interpret all that is said.

Augustine's mother was Monica, for whom the place Santa Monica is named. His father, Patricius, whom he did not like so much, was a member of the council (fifty to one hundred men who could be elected to office in the city), but this did not mean great wealth. When Augustine had to interrupt his studies because of his father's financial problems, he was helped by a wealthy landowner, Romanianus, whose son later became Augustine's pupil in Italy. After studying in Carthage, he taught grammar in Thagaste, then rhetoric to sons of the upper classes in Carthage and later in Rome.

He was on a successful path, and his pious mother encouraged his upward mobility. But he developed other aspirations as well. In his nineteenth year, he says, he read Cicero's *Hortensius* and was aroused to the life of philosophy, the quest for wisdom. This, he suggests, was the moment when he stopped bending his neck to the yoke of authority. The restless and indeterminate quest of the human spirit is evoked at the beginning of the *Confessions*: "You have made us for yourself, and our hearts are restless till they rest in you."[2] Yes, God is the answer. But that answer is not packed into human nature; the quest may explore many possibilities and still not arrive at the answer.

Convinced that he should follow the path of reason, he turned away from the authoritarianism of the Catholic Church in North Africa. Yet he always thought of himself as Christian in some sense, and Monica kept reinforcing this. He mentions that one liaison—probably with his concubine of fourteen years—began in church.[3] In one of the recently discovered sermons he recalls that, prior to the separation of the sexes in church, he engaged in what we would call "inappropriate touching."[4]

Readers often scold Augustine for leaving the concubine nameless. But he does the same with the dying friend.[5] It is not that they are unimportant. Perhaps he was protecting the reputation of the concubine, who was still alive; since Augustine says that she "vowed to God that she would know no other man," she was probably living as a nun.[6] Their namelessness is rhetorically more effective, creating a textual mystery, perhaps a textual wound. It should be noted that even Monica and Patricius are named only once, in the last chapter of Book IX. To be named in this text is not necessarily a sign of emotive intimacy.

He fell in with the Manichaeans, who claimed to base their religion on reason rather than authority. He adopted it as a more enlightened form of Christianity (later he decided that it was myth masquerading as natural science). He had started with the religious beliefs of a provincial, strongly influenced by the simple faith of his mother. Now he identified with Carthaginian and then Roman intellectuals and looked for a more sophisticated set of beliefs.

When the position of city orator in Milan opened up, he applied for it and performed a trial oration before Symmachus, prefect of Rome. The move occurred in the fall of 384, only a few months after the pamphlet war between Symmachus and Bishop Ambrose over the removal of the Altar of Victory (the personified goddess Victoria) from the Senate chambers in Rome. The battle sounds familiar today; it corresponds almost exactly with our disputes over displaying the Ten Commandments in courtrooms. To the emperor Gratian it meant secularizing the functions of government to avoid offending either Christians or pagans (he was following the policy set by Constantine, one of the inventors of religious freedom). To Symmachus it meant abandonment of public support for traditional religious values. Symmachus was probably glad to find an orator who did not belong to the Catholic camp, and Augustine was willing to play a part in the religious wars of the time—on the side of tolerance and pluralism, including diverse modes of Christian belief, not of paganism. Later Augustine would develop, at the end of *The City of God*, his own theory of the secular state as distinct from the church.

Augustine was hoping for appointment to an imperial office, and his mother arranged a marriage suitable to a person with such aspirations. But he also encountered a group of intellectuals, some of them high officials in the court, who were interested in the writings of the Platonists. For them the attractions of Platonism seemed to be as strong as those of public life; perhaps they had misgivings about the flattery that is always part of official life, and they were certainly aware of the grim fate of colleagues who fell from favor.

During Holy Week in 386 there was confrontation in Milan between Ambrose and Justina, regent for the young emperor Valentinian II, who wanted to turn over one of the churches to the Arians (mostly Gothic mercenaries). When Ambrose and his supporters occupied the basilica in protest, it was surrounded by Gothic troops with their long hair and mustaches; they became steadily more sympathetic with the protesters. To keep his followers occupied and raise their spirits, Ambrose organized the antiphonal chanting of psalms and composed some metrical hymns (about ten to fifteen of them survive). Although Augustine mentions the episode and says that his mother was there, he was more preoccupied with his own intellectual and spiritual quest than with the politics of doctrine. But the confrontation may have demonstrated the weaknesses of the imperial court—and the strengths of Ambrose and the Catholic Church.

He comments that he was like those wanderers who remember their homeland but delay, gazing at the stars, roaming in the mists, hearing the enticements of sirens. Physically he had been traveling north; now, he says, he looked north figuratively, too, and began to learn about a more credible guide, a Big Dipper pointing to the Pole Star. In a narrative written soon after his conversion he emphasizes three things, which correspond roughly with Books VI, VII, and VIII of the *Confessions*: conversations with the bishop Ambrose, reading some "books of the Platonists," and reading the apostle Paul.[7]

In the first phase, he learned to acknowledge the constructive role of authority, which to the Romans meant relying on the testimony of those who are better acquainted with something true or good. He says he had been imbued with the Christian religion from infancy but was repelled by its dogmatism. When he arrived in Milan he made a courtesy call on Ambrose, the bishop who had just been engaged in controversy with Symmachus; and Ambrose, he says, "received me like a father"—a better one than Patricius and one with whom Monica already had a spiritual relationship. In a few more months he enrolled as a catechumen, having decided to adhere to Catholic Christianity unless something better appeared.

But this by itself was not enough. Subjection to authority might be good enough for simple believers, but not for someone who had been ignited with the philosophic quest. Belief, which is based on authority, does indeed point toward the goal. Faith may even arrive ahead of reason, as Monica, the simple believer, frequently does in the dialogues written soon after Augustine's conversion. But it is better to make belief the beginning of a journey taken by reason, for the goal is to possess truth directly. Now another decisive factor enters the picture.

The second stage is reading what Augustine calls "a few books of the Platonists," and these certainly included several treatises from Plotinus's *Enneads*. In this stage Augustine was converted to Platonism, although under Christian auspices; later, after some weeks or months, he would be fully converted to Christianity, with Platonist overtones. The

Christianity with which he grew up had been intellectually inadequate, driving him into a long detour; now he came to see things in a new light, for Platonism had significant similarities with Christian doctrine.

But the "books of the Platonists" did not resolve his problems; they created a new difficulty. He says repeatedly, in passages coming from all stages of his literary career, that one can glimpse the divine Light shining on one's mind but is immediately driven back, unable to endure it because one's affections are tied to lesser things (only the pure in heart shall see God, says Matt 5:8). He discovered his need for divine assistance, and this was to remain a major theme throughout his life.[8] From this perspective, philosophers like Plotinus and Porphyry were a major example of pride, thinking they could achieve union with God by their own powers. At the end of Book VII Augustine comments that it is one thing to view the homeland from a hilltop, and another thing to get there, since the road is beset with fears and temptations aroused by the rebel angels; one needs the help of Christ the heavenly commander, who gained that role by first humbling himself and becoming incarnate.

In the third stage he finally gets underway. Soon after the event, he mentions two motivating factors: the attraction of the religion that had been grafted into him as a child and the powerful example of actual lives. Marius Victorinus, translator of the "books of the Platonists" that Augustine read in Milan and a professor of rhetoric in Rome whose baptism created a public stir, was a model worth emulating. Then there was Antony the Egyptian monk, whose *Life*, written by Athanasius, had already influenced many others. Farther back, he may have been thinking of those two nameless figures in the *Confessions*: the friend who reproached Augustine by receiving Catholic baptism before he died, and the concubine, who, earlier than himself, vowed "to God" that she would live in chastity and, thus, was more faithful than he to their virtual marriage.[9]

But the decisive moment, according to the *Confessions*, came when he read a passage in Paul's Letter to the Romans. The account in the *Confessions* is not straightforward narrative; it is so full of imagery that scholars have trouble distinguishing fact from interpretation. A year before writing the *Confessions* he had come to the theory that God's grace acts upon the human affections through "suggestions" that occur to us (see ch. 5); now the theory shapes the narrative, which is different from his telling of the story in the months after his conversion.

In this passage he briefly states his theory of willing. He calls attention to a *monstrum*, a strange phenomenon: when the mind commands the body it is obeyed, but when it commands itself it is not obeyed. The solution is not that there are two souls, as the Manichaeans thought; it is that our affections are divided, so that the desire to change is only halfhearted and is counterbalanced by what we are already accustomed to.[10] He tells how his "old loves" plucked at his garment of flesh to keep him from going down a different path, to which he was beckoned by "Continence and her children." But only the divine call frees the will to act wholeheartedly.

How, then, does it happen? Just as Antony was converted by hearing a passage from scripture, Augustine is converted by reading another passage, and his friend Alypius by reading a third. Each person is addressed in a way that fits his own needs, that "speaks to his condition." In Augustine's case it was a passage in Romans: "not in reveling and drunkenness, not in chambering and wantonness, not in quarreling and jealousy. But put on the Lord Jesus Christ, and make no provision for the flesh, to gratify its desires" (Rom 13:13-14). He read it not with guilt or shame, but as advice and promise. It looked to him, the philosopher, like a classification of the three kinds of vice and an indication of the way to overcome them.

Augustine and his friends, and his mother Monica, went on retreat in the fall, in Cassiciacum in the hills north of Milan; he reported their conversations in several dialogues in which Augustine is the controlling figure, the new Socrates or Cicero. He returned to Milan, took instruction during Lent, and was baptized at Easter in 387. After Monica's death in Ostia, the port of Rome, he returned to Thagaste and set up a philosophic/monastic community.

A few years later, it was through the monastic life that Augustine, against his intentions, stumbled into the clergy. He had avoided any place without a bishop, but in the winter of 390/91, seeking out a friend who had expressed interest in his community, he came to Hippo Regius, whose Greek-born bishop was aging. When he entered the church he was recognized and was forcibly detained to become a presbyter and bishop-designate.

He would have preferred contemplation; now he accepts the "active life" of a churchman. Within the space of four years he had lost Monica, his friends Verecundus and Nebridius, and his son Adeodatus; links with his past had been forcibly broken. Perhaps it was to suggest the gap between then and now that he ended his autobiographical narrative in the *Confessions* with Monica's death, ten years before the time of writing.

Now he finds a new family in the community of the church in Hippo and the monastery he founds next to it. He begins a new career with very different responsibilities—and definitely to our benefit, for his public becomes much broader than the educated intellectuals for whom he had been writing. For a few years in the 390s he seems to have experienced "writer's block," starting several works and then abandoning them.[11] After he became a bishop in 395/96, he found his voice, pouring out a steady flow of sermons, letters, and books until his death in 430. He was not any less an intellectual; works like *On the Trinity* and *The City of God* are proof of that. But now he was an intellectual in a quite different mode.

He was still a master of Latin writing and rhetoric; but he also composed an alphabetical psalm in popular style to combat the Donatists. He now viewed his early, more philosophical works as pretentious. He identified with the Christian community, adopting the custom of addressing the congregation with the honorific "Your Charity" (a reversal of "Your Majesty" and "Your Holiness"). He had the constant burden of hearing personal disputes, one of the legal innovations made by Constantine. In one sermon he notes that many wealthy and powerful people still took the attitude, "If I become a Christian I will be like my doorkeeper."[12] Christian clergy wore the simple tunic that was also worn by farmers and artisans—somewhat like the turtleneck sweater of the French worker priests. In one sermon there is a dramatic passage that would be quoted by the Second Vatican Council:

> While I am terrified of what I am *for* you, I am consoled by what I am *with* you. *For* you I am a bishop, *with* you I am a Christian. The former is the name of an office assumed, the latter is the name of a grace received; the former means danger, the latter salvation.[13]

More consistently than before, he lived like a citizen of the heavenly city of God, sojourning in the earthly city.

Augustine did not abandon the "contemplative life" when he added to it the "active life" of a bishop. He continued the monastery that he had started in 391 near the basilica, encouraging all the clergy to live together in the "common life," and he wrote a rule based on the Sermon on the Mount and the early Christian community (Acts 2:44-45; 4:32 and 35). He always regarded the monastic community as the closest earthly approximation to the heavenly city of God. It had all things "in common," both in turning away from private property (since seeking one's own, the *proprium*, a changeable self trying to control changeable things, leads only to deprivation, the *privatum*) and in adhering to God as the one in whom all are united.[14]

A crucial shift in his expectations came at this time. He had thought it possible to achieve a constant vision of God through intellectual exercise and self-discipline. He now decides that this must be deferred: happiness is gained only "in hope" (*in spe*), not "in reality" (*in re*); the

Christian is described as a sojourner, a wanderer away from home (cf. 2 Cor 5:6), "reaching forward" toward a different future (cf. Phil 3:13). This meant that the inner life is one of faith, hope, and love, not vision. If there is an immediate relationship with God, it is through love rather than knowledge.

The opaqueness of the body was an increasing problem to him, part of the pathos of the human condition. It is not only that we cannot behold God, we cannot behold each other's minds either. Without communication and mutual trust there would be no home and family, no agriculture, no living together in cities. But when we depend on communication, there is also the possibility of lying and simulated friendship. Both comedy and tragedy are often built on deception or misunderstanding. In our own day we are concerned about "transparency" in government and business. We would rather believe what people say than have no friends at all. But truth is important, and Augustine was unique in the ancient world—with its noble lies, pious forgeries, and image-making—for insisting on truth-telling under all circumstances.[15] (One is not obliged to tell *all* that one knows; one can say or do things *pedagogically*, as Jesus often did, so that others will arrive at the truth by themselves; and others may erroneously *interpret* what is said or done.) Increasingly he looked forward to the situation after death, "when the Lord comes, illuminating the things now hidden in darkness and disclosing the thoughts of the heart" (1 Cor 4:5).

As a bishop, Augustine had to direct his attention to the outward world, not only to the church but to the empire. In some ways it was a reversal of the journey inward that occurred in 386, the year of his conversion, when he, like the group in Milan that included some high officials, turned away from public life toward contemplation.

It was a particularly rewarding time for attending to external affairs. During the 390s the political situation changed drastically. The emperor Theodosius, a Spaniard, had received baptism in 380 (previous emperors, even those sympathetic to Christianity, had been baptized only when they were near death). Starting in 380 he enforced the Nicene doctrine of the Trinity; he also outlawed Manichaeism (this may have been one factor in Augustine's detaching himself from that movement). In 394, in a battle in the valley of the Frigidus in what is now Slovenia, near Trieste, he defeated a rival emperor (a Christian, but a tolerant one) under what seemed to be miraculous circumstances. Theodosius and his sons now had an excuse to ban sacrifices, smash idols, and convert temples into churches. One of the ironies of history is that the Greek temples that survive are the ones turned into Christian churches around the year 400.

For four centuries there had been a life-and-death struggle between Christianity and paganism; now the Christians, after many reversals, were the victors, and their attitude was, in effect, "never again." Christians writing histories of the church considered this a time of fulfillment and closure, far more satisfying than the age of Constantine. To Augustine these years fulfilled the prophecies that rulers would serve God, and God's name would be praised from the rising to the setting of the sun. Part of that fulfillment, of course, was government suppression of paganism and idolatry and government pressure on dissident Christian movements such as the Donatists and the Pelagians.

Those are topics that will be discussed later. For the present, we return to the "contemplative" Augustine of the early dialogues.

Questions for Reflection

1. The Greco-Roman world had many philosophical and religious options, and Augustine explored a number of them. What options encounter us in our own time? How have you been influenced by them? How have you come to your own resolution of them (if at all)?

2. Augustine adjusted his perspectives a number of times, not only before but after his conversion. Why? Was he overly impressionable, blown by one wind after another, or is there a basic continuity through it all?

CHAPTER TWO

REASON'S QUEST: AUGUSTINE THE PLATONIST

Augustine's encounter with Platonism offered him a framework within which to understand Christian doctrine. It would remain the framework of his thought from start to finish, still expressed in passages from his last decade. He revised or corrected Platonism at a number of points, however, to bring it into harmony with Christian teaching. And within this framework his thinking became increasingly more complex as he encountered new issues raised by the biblical tradition and his concerns shifted from contemplation to pastoral care for all sorts and conditions of people.

There had been Platonist overtones in Christianity from the start. Stephen's speech in Acts 7 allegorizes the rituals of the law and says that the "temple built with hands" is inferior to the spiritual worship that God really wants, based on "the pattern Moses had seen on the mount" (Exod 25:9 and 40; Acts 7:44). To someone who knew Plato's *Timaeus*, that must be the "pattern," the *paradeigma*, the intelligible realm according to which God created and governed all things, far surpassing earthly rituals and buildings. Philo, the Jewish philosopher in Alexandria, had already floated this interpretation among cosmopolitan Jews.

Platonism became central to Christian theology with Justin Martyr, whose writings come from the period 150–180. He picked up from the Stoics the notion of the divine Word as cosmic reason, and this seemed similar both to Plato's "intelligible world" and to Gen 1, where God speaks and gives form to matter. The Word of God, he said, illuminates all people, including the Greek philosophers, but in a partial and fragmentary way; the Word becomes fully present in Jesus Christ, who enables people to know God, lead virtuous lives, and defy the demons, who are the instigators of pagan religion.

Justin asserts, therefore, that the Christians are the only ones who really live up to the philosophers' own principles. Socrates sacrificed a rooster just before his death; educated people went along with polytheism and participated in the civic sacrifices even when they were open skeptics; and they were careful not to offend the demons, who could be placated through incantations and smoky sacrifices. Augustine makes the same argument: if Plato and others were to reappear, they would acknowledge that this is the way of life they glimpsed as the right one, but they did not have the courage of their own convictions.[1]

Christianity was provocative in many ways, telling Jews that the hoped-for ingathering of the Gentiles had come and telling Gentiles that they must live up to their own best principles. Christian writers often gloated about the number of Gentiles who abandoned the religion of their cities or their ethnic groups and turned toward the truth. As Gibbon pointed out, "The Jews were a people which followed, the Christians a sect which deserted, the religion of their fathers."[2] One reason they were able to do this is that they laid claim to the moral and metaphysical authority of the philosophers, which in the ancient world could trump both popular religion and government authority. Even persecution could be a recommendation, for there had been philosophers, too, who sacrificed their lives for their principles.

That is the general context that prevailed "from Justin to Augustine." Now we turn specifically to the Cassiciacum dialogues, written during the few months between Augustine's conversion and his baptism. In them he deals with several sets of questions, moving from one to another and back again. Scholars disagree about the exact sequence of the discussions (if the written dialogues even reflect what was actually said), but the process was a circular one.

He begins with the quest for happiness. In Greek culture it was usual to say that all people desire happiness. (Ethical theory calls this position *eudaemonism*, and it is contrasted with other views that emphasize rules or consequences or responsiveness to values.) But this is only a generalized desire; we do not know *what* will give happiness.

From Cicero, the main carrier of Greek philosophy into the Roman world, Augustine got some useful guidelines. In his *Hortensius*, the work Augustine read at the age of nineteen, Cicero said that we seek what is *worth having*, and is *attainable*, and *with security*, without fear of losing it against one's will. He adds some cautions: we should not seek *whatever* delights us or think that happiness consists in gaining *whatever* we desire, for we cannot be happy in possessing something *inappropriate* to human fulfillment.[3] Philosophers went through the whole list of possibilities: money, power, pleasure, and so on, all of which are used up in the enjoyment and can be lost to someone else.

Given this prescription, Plato and Aristotle and many others were convinced that true happiness is found only in contemplating God; and this, of course, was welcomed by Christian thinkers as one more sign that the philosophers were on the right track, thanks to God's light shining on all. The happiness that comes from contemplation is enduring and secure. The object is not used up in the process of enjoyment; neither must it be divided up and allocated, for all can share in the same fulfillment without rivalry, the more the better. God is loved for God's own sake, not as a means to one's own fulfillment. Cupidity, by contrast, is the self-centered love of things that can be lost against one's will, making one not only unhappy but *unwillingly* unhappy.

Augustine was criticized by Anders Nygren in his often-cited book *Agape and Eros.* Drawing a contrast between Greek *eros* (desiring love) and Christian *agape* (altruistic love), he thought that Augustine's "*caritas* synthesis" was not a satisfactory resolution.[4] Nygren's position has been challenged by many: first by John Burnaby,[5] then by several contributors to a retrospective analysis of Nygren's thought.[6] The issue is this: if human beings find happiness in the contemplation of God, it appears that God is being used as a means to human fulfillment. For Augustine, however, human fulfillment is found in the appreciation of God for God's own sake, because God is other than and more valuable than oneself. There were similar confusions during the Middle Ages. Some thought in terms of a "natural" desire for God for the sake of human fulfillment; others thought of love as entirely self-abandoning. The resolution, once again, was that genuine fulfillment is found in treasuring and enjoying God for God's own sake and through the grace of God. The aesthetic experience of beauty has often been seen as the closest parallel.

Anyone who has read Plotinus will know how persuasively he evokes the rosy glow of a realm that can be entered through contemplation. Beauty, he says, is apparent even to the senses. But then one sees that this beauty comes from harmony, form, idea. With the eye of the soul one seeks communion with an intelligible realm, freeing oneself of bodily senses and desires. It is a journey not of the feet, not of ships or chariots, but of a soul that must purify itself, becoming like that which it seeks to behold.[7]

When Augustine read Plotinus, he experienced a combination of delight and discomfiture. He tells how, in a flash, he glimpsed the divine Light; but immediately he was driven back by its splendor, unable to endure its presence. "I saw that there was something to see," he says, "but I was not yet the one to see it."[8] The task, then, was to free the soul's wings from all that holds them down. Through spiritual exercises, he thought, he could achieve that vision. In fact, his hope was to enjoy that vision uninterruptedly so that his life, even in the body, would be a "life in happiness," contemplating eternal things and minimizing concern with finite things. As he says in the *Confessions*, he wanted not only to *see* but to *dwell in* this realm.[9]

This is what Plotinus had shown him. But the experience of his own inability led him to criticize the philosophers for their pride in thinking they could accomplish it by their own wisdom and their own powers. He also faulted the philosophers for setting themselves apart from the majority of people, who must content themselves with lesser kinds of religion, which the philosophers held in contempt. Faith, Augustine said, is needed by all, and for two reasons: to complete an imperfect awareness of the transcendent God and to learn about this God's free acts for human salvation. It did not mean, at least for him, remaining in simple faith; one who has been fired by the philosophic quest must keep using reason. But even that person must start with faith, just like the common people.

For him, then, faith is a stage on reason's journey, for the goal is to possess truth directly, through reason. The expression "faith seeking understanding" is typically Augustinian; he often quotes the Old Latin mistranslation of Isa 7:9, "Unless you believe you will not understand." In this connection he makes three basic points: reason acting on its own will be frustrated; reason's path must begin with faith; and after it does so, it can rise above mere faith and achieve a more lucid understanding. Augustine has been understood as a fideist, a rationalist, and a mystic; in fact he has something of all three.

Before reason sets out on its journey, however, it is necessary to demonstrate that reason can follow a path such as this. A turning point in Augustine's intellectual pilgrimage had come when he read in Cicero about the critical theory of knowledge advocated by the "New Academy." This led him to question Manichaeism with its claims to tangible knowledge of good and evil substances. But it also brought uncertainty as to whether reason is able to accomplish much of anything.

The background is this: Plato was the founder of the Academy in Athens; but under Carneades, in the second century B.C.E., the Academy adopted the position that truth is unattainable, since every proof requires another proof, in infinite regress. (This sounds very much like Derrida's *différance*, indefinite deferral; and it is a challenge that must always be taken seriously.) In the history of philosophy, "*Platonism*" has come to mean the teachings in Plato's dialogues; "the Academics" applies to this newer perspective of critical doubt.

We should remind ourselves that *doubt* properly means hesitation, not negation; we doubt "whether," not "that." The Academics counseled suspension of judgment, withholding of assent. They were dealing with a genuine problem. An oar in water appears bent. No deception is involved; light is simply following its own nature, and the eyes do their proper work. The error is in the judgment, "That oar is bent."[10] At best, they argued, we can gain "verisimilitude," likeness to truth, since appearances must manifest something even when it remains unknown. In practical affairs, where we must decide to do something definite, probability was their guide.

This is certainly one feature of human experience. A now-classic expression is Joni Mitchell's 1969 song "Both Sides, Now." Each verse evokes the shifting and multivalent character of clouds, then of love, then of life. The first refrain concludes, "I really don't know clouds at all." The same applies to love, and to life.

Augustine resolved the apparent conflict within the Platonist tradition in this way: the New Academy, he said, was a legitimate extension of the Old Academy, taking the critical role of questioning mere appearance and pointing out the shifting and unstable character of sense experience; in so doing it prepared the way for Plato's more esoteric teaching, that truth, guidance, and happiness are to be found in an intelligible realm.

In *On the Academics*, one of the Cassiciacum dialogues, Augustine plays the two realms against each other. Those who think they have grasped truth through the senses find that it slips away like the mythic Proteus, who could never be held down. Augustine is confident, however, that Proteus is really the divine truth that can be found by other means. How, then, can certitude be gained?

One argument is from *presupposition*. Even if one denies wisdom or truth, wisdom or truth is still what makes this judgment possible. To speak of "verisimilitude" is to assume something about truth, if only as a goal that recedes infinitely. Augustine did not claim too much here. While he did indeed affirm that God is wisdom and truth, he always acknowledged, for the sake of argument, alternative possibilities. If truth cannot be attained, one should be happy in seeking it without illusion or error. If there is a diversity of goals, wisdom still has insight into them. If happiness cannot be attained, virtue's struggle is better than being dominated by vice.[11]

His most important argument looks at *reflexivity*. Just as *word* refers to other words but also circles back and refers to itself as a word, so the mind, which is capable of apprehending many things, knows itself. The most influential argument is from *doubt*. Augustine formulated it not at Cassiciacum but many years later: "I doubt, therefore I am."[12] In this, of course, he anticipated Descartes, one of the founders of modern philosophy. If we assume nothing about external reality, Descartes said, and turn inward, we can gain certitude from self-awareness, starting with the truth, "I think, therefore I am." Seventeenth-century Augustinians welcomed Descartes' writings, since he, like Augustine, emphasized "God and the soul," showing that Augustine was a genuine and profound philosopher.

Note that these arguments do not conclude to a Platonic realm of intelligibles; they simply trace the operations of the human mind, and their purpose is to help the mind understand itself so that it might become capable of a direct vision of divine truth. The divine is reached not through argument but through a process of initiation into immediate intuition.

Plotinus had urged the soul to know itself and learn that its eye is capable of seeing God, to seek a solitude uninterrupted by externals so that it might look and see God.[13] Augustine heard Christian resonances in this. The prodigal son, after going to the "far country" (Luke 15:13 RSV), eventually "came to himself" (Luke 15:17 RSV) and decided to return to his true home. It is not a matter of spatial change; the problem is that the mind's attention has gone outside itself. The situation, Augustine says (addressing God), is that "you were within, and I was outside . . . you were with me, but I was not with you."[14] God is *"interior intimo meo,"* more inward than my own inwardness.[15]

Note the similarities with our contemporary interest in meditation, often described as "centering." In one sense the centering is valuable in itself, achieving rest from the sensory overload of ordinary experience and the dissipating effect of concern with external things; often this is the extent of contemporary "spirituality." But it is usually understood as a stage on the way toward experience of God, mediated or immediate.

Augustine learned two important things from Plotinus. First, omnipresence became one of God's most important attributes. God is "everywhere entire"; "all of God is everywhere," not localized or divided, fully available to those who are able to become aware of God.[16] Second, he sought immediate awareness of God with "nothing between."[17] This could find some surprising applications. When Augustine read Paul's statement that "nothing in all creation" can separate us from the love of God (Rom 8:39), he reflected that the human mind, while it is one of the created things, ought not to be separated from God by love of other created things; in that sense, then, there ought to be "nothing between" the mind and God.[18]

In this connection we should take note of another characteristically Augustinian interpretation of Paul. When Paul says that the invisible things of God are "understood by being seen through the things that are made" (Rom 1:20), Augustine always interprets this to mean not "proofs" for God's existence through a reasoning process but a turning within and then above oneself; it happens "through" the things that are made in the sense that both the outward and the inward become springboards for looking upward.

Perhaps the most impressive example of this process is Book VI of Augustine's work *On Music*, where he discusses "numbers" or proportions, starting with the physical sounds and moving inward to hearing, memory, the spontaneous judgments that arouse "delight" at these proportions, and finally to the intelligible principles by which such judgments are made. It is a progression from acoustics to physiology and psychology and finally to metaphysics and mysticism.

Having dealt with the more personal and religious aspects of the Platonist tradition, which were certainly more important to Augustine, we must come to a closely related topic that was less urgent but seemed to give intellectual reinforcement to his quest for initiation into the presence of God.

Augustine as a Platonist was certain that there is an intelligible realm of ideas. He began from experience: the human mind judges sensory things, which are *beneath* itself; it judges in accordance with norms or ideals that are *above* the judging mind. The question is how the mind becomes aware of those norms.

He usually speaks of "illumination" by the divine Word. But it is not entirely clear how this is to be understood; this is one of many topics over which scholars continue to disagree. It is not that everything is known and understood "in God," as though earthbound and sinful minds have an immediate vision of God. It is not, as some medieval philosophers thought, that God implants all concepts in our minds, filling the function of Aristotle's "agent intellect" that confers abstract intelligibles on the mind, for Augustine knows that the human mind is not only distinct from divine mind but has its own role in abstracting and reasoning.

If Augustine is confident that the divine Light is always shining upon the mind, he knows that we are most likely to become aware of it when we are reasoning and judging about other things. He uses terms like *memory* or, more clearly, *notion* (based on *nosse*, "having known"), to suggest that illumination is *presupposed* by the more explicit operations of the mind. Divine illumination acts like the sun, conferring intelligibility even when it is not directly seen. It functions as the background or basis or legitimation for intellectual operations, a dimension of ultimacy.

To Augustine, rational certitude is an important step on the way toward God. He would like to be as sure about God as he is about mathematical truths. But there is considerable difference between the two. To see the light of a fire from the distance is not to enjoy its warmth up close; to be an accountant able to use numbers is not to be a wise person.[19] The similarity between knowing mathematics and knowing God is that the path to be followed is not a way of demonstrations or proofs but of *recognition*.

So the argument is this: just as we say that three plus seven *is* ten (not *must be* ten, as though we have power over them), similarly in thinking about God we do not say that God *must be* but that God *is*, for God is Being in its fullness. Not even God, he adds, judges truth, for the Word of God *is* Truth.[20] We are on the way toward Anselm, whose ontological

18

argument was an attempt to go through faith to certitude. Faith moves *toward* God, confident that God is always the same, perfect, neither vulnerable to change nor in need of fulfillment; by contrast, understanding, which is more than faith, moves *from* God, for it has discovered that God, as Being in its fullness, *cannot not be.* This is not a logical demonstration but a process of personal initiation, and the argument will be convincing only when we move from, not to, its conclusion.

What are we to say about all of this? Philosophers have always argued about the nature and validity of the ontological argument; they have argued even more about the nature of the intelligibles that are part of our mental experience. Criticism has reached a new intensity in our own time.

Augustine the Platonist is named as a major instance of what is called the "metaphysics of presence" by its critics, most notably Heidegger and Derrida. They agree with Augustine that human life is temporal and beset with constant change. But they question all attempts to rise above temporality. Augustine, they say, seeks a presence that is nontemporal, immediately accessible, fixed, independent of the mind, "recognized" rather than created or conceptualized by the mind. To him, the immediacy and self-evidence of intelligible truths manifested a different and higher realm; to his critics, it is merely an example of *logocentrism.* They are like the New Academy questioning the Old Academy of Platonist dogma.

Perhaps even more damaging is Foucault's linking of knowledge with power. The paradigm of modern science and medicine, he says, is "the examination." Here only the person subjected to examination is made visible. The examiner and the norms of judgment become invisible, abstract, transcendent, static, universal. That means that the one being examined is more individual, particular, and thus "less normal."[21]

We can see the point of these attempts to deconstruct Platonism. But we must also ask whether, or to what extent, Augustine falls into the hands of his critics.

He did indeed think in terms of "presence." God is omnipresent, and "all of God is everywhere," even when not apprehended. But it is not an inert or passive presence in the way abstractions seem to be present to the mind. Aristotle scored a point in his critique of self-subsisting ideas floating above the world; for him all intelligibles are in mind. The so-called Middle Platonists took his critique seriously and spoke of the ideas as thoughts in divine mind. When it came to illumination, Augustine did not think of God's presence as inert or abstract, somehow "there" to be seen. He thinks of presence as an active "presenting"; the divine Light is constantly shining on the eye of the mind. God is, to be sure, always the same—but *actively* the same, fully actual, Being Itself.

19

Alternatives to his position deserve examination. When Augustine pointed to the obvious fact that judgments are made in accordance with norms that are "above" the judging mind, he was not aware of non-Euclidean geometries, the diversity of linguistic systems, or the social and cultural construction of reality. He did acknowledge the striking differences among moral codes, even within the biblical tradition, but he was certain that God's standard of justice presides over them all.[22]

For him the importance of mathematical truths and moral norms was that they are not subjective, do not make a merely private claim, for they can be apprehended by all as shared objects of awareness. This indicates a crucial difference between his age and ours. Then, what seemed most significant about agreed truths and values is that they are *the same for all*; now, it is that they are *shared*, and our question is *why* they are agreed upon, for we know that they are unlikely to be shared by *all* persons *everywhere*. The irony is that Augustine said much the same thing in his critique of human culture in the "earthly city," where agreement is based on desire and compulsion.[23] But he was convinced that this can be transcended through reflection and the quest for unchanging truth and justice.

When our age asks about the transcendental conditions for intelligibility and persuasiveness, the first question is not likely to be about objective norms but about communication and readiness to understand each other, then about the rival claims of truth and value that are made, and then about the ways these might be validated. Sometimes they are validated through observation, sometimes through practical results (psychological, social, technological), sometimes through their comprehensiveness and fruitfulness. It is still reason's quest. But reason is faced with many paths, and its way toward satisfaction, perhaps even toward happiness, is as winding as Augustine at some moments acknowledged it to be.

Questions for Reflection

1. Why does Augustine assert that (a) belief comes before understanding, and yet that (b) it is a stage on reason's way and that (c) understanding can rise beyond mere belief?

2. One of the attractions of Platonism is its awareness of the need for "spiritual exercises" through "centering" and "inwardness." But there have always been those who insist that it claims too much about reaching God. What considerations count for and against Augustine's brand of Platonism?

CHAPTER THREE

WHY EVIL? ANSWERING THE MANICHAEANS

A ugustine took evil seriously. Manichaeism had appealed to him because it, too, took evil seriously, both within ourselves and in the world. It thought of evil as a tangible force: evil is that within ourselves that makes us do the wrong things, and in nature it is the cause of suffering and death. On this view, evil is easily contrasted with good and is in clearly recognizable struggle with it.

The founder, Mani (216–277), was born in Mesopotamia. He claimed to complete and unify several religious traditions—Christian, Zoroastrian, and Buddhist—and sent missionaries into both the Mediterranean world and Central Asia. Manichaeism's appeal in the West was as a more reasonable form of Christianity, one that emphasized Paul and rejected the Old Testament as the product of an alien deity. According to its myth, good and evil began as separate realms. Then evil, fascinated by good, invaded it; to halt this invasion, some of the good forces were sacrificed, becoming the nuclei around which the present world was able to gain coherence. (Augustine's philosophically inclined friend Nebridius posed a dilemma: if the forces of good could not be harmed by the forces of evil, why did they go into a damaging combat with them?[1]) The Manichaeans viewed the glow of sexual delight as a trick by which good is kept in captivity, generation after generation; the task, then, was to free the particles of light through sexual abstinence (or at least by ensuring that intercourse did not lead to conception) and a complex set of dietary practices. The human struggle was a microcosm of the cosmic conflict.

For a decade and more after his conversion, Augustine wrote a series of anti-Manichaean works. Against their dualism he developed an alternative theory of evil; against their fatalistic view that sin comes from an "evil nature" within oneself he insisted on freedom of choice; and against their rejection of the Old Testament he argued that the grace of God has been active from the beginning of human history and is manifested in the events and ceremonies of ancient Israel.

Today we often talk about "Manichaean politics." It is the habit of identifying an "evil empire" or an "axis of evil" in countries that can be named, then going to war to "exterminate evil." But we may have second thoughts. This looks disturbingly like the "scapegoating violence" analyzed in recent decades by René Girard: we have all sorts of rivalries with each other, and conflict is avoided by focusing the blame upon a precise target, on the fiction that "everything would be all right among us if it weren't for so and so."[2] The easiest targets are the poor, the vulnerable, and foreigners. Punishment of criminals often has features of ritual purgation; lynching is a more horrendous and more revealing example. But the target can also be those who are in power, especially when a rival candidate is waiting in the wings, and then there can be an even more satisfying feeling of judgment, revenge, and closure as dictators are killed and their statues are toppled. Charles I of England was beheaded at the instigation of Cromwell's New Model Army; but the Presbyterians opposed it. The French king Louis XVI was guillotined at the insistence of Robespierre; but Tom Paine, the Revolutionary hero, was there and opposed it, almost being guillotined himself. After Calvin and the Genevans burned Servetus for heresy concerning the Trinity, Sebastian Castellio threw cold water on their achievement, saying, "They did not defend a doctrine; they killed a man." Examples like these raise the question of how well evil can be eradicated through violence.

If evil is not a tangible thing, a component in the world that is opposed to the good, and if we cannot get rid of it by attacking an identifiable target, what is the alternative?

The so-called privation theory says that evil, whether it is evil *done* or evil *suffered*, is always a corruption or lack of something good. What we call evil in nature is death, suffering, diminishment. What is evil for the prey is good for the carnivore. All things interact, supporting each other through symbiosis, yes, but also competing with each other and preying on each other all the way up and down the food chain. We reintroduce wolves into Yellowstone to restore the "balance of nature," which we, like Augustine, regard as "good."

Augustine compared this balance of good and evil in the natural world with the contrasts in a tile floor, where the dark parts contribute to the harmony of the whole (since the Renaissance we would be more likely to compare it with a chiaroscuro painting). In one classic statement he expressed the conviction that God permits evil because God also knows how to bring good out of it.[3] When he interpreted the psalms that complain about the sufferings of the righteous and the prosperity of the wicked, his rule of thumb was that providence is evident enough to convince us that God cares for the world, but suffering is allowed to continue so that we will hope for something better. Life may seem to be unfair from a restricted point of view; there is justice when we view the whole picture.

Augustine is not passive toward evil. We may be able to change our situation by using science, medicine, and technology. He compared life in the world to visiting a forge, where we are surrounded by dangerous implements but the smith knows how to use them constructively.[4] Human interactions may be full of tragedy, and this is evoked with sensitivity and eloquence in great literature; but Augustine warns us to be careful. In his youth, he recalls, he mourned the death of Dido (a major episode in Virgil's *Aeneid*) but not his own spiritual death;[5] he thinks that the problem with tragedy is that it calls on us merely to feel sad, not to help those who suffer.[6] He might have liked Bertolt Brecht's theory that the purpose of drama is not emotional catharsis but agitation, making a difference in the real world.

A classic exposition of his theory of "moral evil" is in Book II of the *Confessions*, where he asks why he stole pears during his adolescence. He is not agonizing out of guilt; he is exploring the full range of answers to the question *why*. One, of course, is that evil is done for its own sake. But the final answer is that he did it for the sake of companionship. The implied conclusion is that an evil act is always willed for the sake of some "good," some value, but to the loss, the privation, of some better value. When a child acts up, we say, "He's trying to prove something"—namely his freedom, his ability to do anything he wants to do. Likewise in the case of suicide, Augustine argues that what is willed is not nonexistence as such but peace, rest, the cessation of pain or misery (psychologists in our day add that the motive may be to make others feel sorry for what they have done or not done).

When finite things are loved in disordered or inappropriate ways, the things themselves do not become evil; the evil is in the misdirected love. Several times Augustine says that evil has not an *efficient* but only a *deficient* cause.[7] He is not just being clever. The evil consists in the defection from a better to a worse possibility. And how does this happen? In many ways: distraction, lapse of attention, impulsiveness, fear, selfishness, assertiveness, too narrow a range of vision, too broad a range of vision—in sum, faults of both omission and commission.

Augustine did not invent the privation theory; it was anticipated by many of the Platonists and by several earlier Christian thinkers. Gregory of Nyssa even offered the interesting suggestion that evil finds its own limit: since it is the corruption of something good, it can go only so far; then things "touch bottom" and are ready to be moved in the other direction. But Augustine, of course, is the one who put it on the map for Western culture.

If we say that evil is not a *thing*, then some people object that it is not being taken seriously. But Augustine knew that physical harm, deprivation, and suffering are quite real. He has always astonished readers with his frankness about political evil: "Tear off the disguise of wild delusion; let the crimes be seen naked, weighed naked, judged naked."[8] But he emphasizes what happens inside human beings:

> What is it about war that is blameworthy? Is it that people who will at some time die anyway are killed so that the victor can live in peace? . . . What rightly deserves censure in war is the desire to harm, cruel vengeance, an unappeased and implacable spirit, the savagery of rebellion, lust for domination, and other such things.[9]

He was not thinking merely of bloodthirsty emotions, which can come and go. Hatred is even more dangerous at the level of ideology, which cold-bloodedly justifies such actions by demonizing the opponent and claiming too much righteousness for one's own side. Doing evil is not always as dramatic as this. One strength of the privation theory is that it shows how evil can come from a seemingly trivial lapse of attention, or focusing on some values to the neglect of others, or believing political ideology or spin, or simply "doing one's job." Hannah Arendt got into trouble with other Jews in 1963 when, reporting on the Eichmann trial, she coined the expression "the banality of evil."[10] They finally understood that she was not engaged in Holocaust denial. She was trying to figure out how people could participate in it, and the motivations were not necessarily dramatic. It was enough simply to be a "good German," doing one's duty with efficiency and not asking too many questions.

In recent decades we have learned how pervasive the sense of lack, privation, and defect can be—and how misleading our impressions may be, since they are both subjective and socially constructed. How do we recognize a deficiency, and when is it evil?

Difference easily comes to mean inferiority or deficiency; then deprivation and cruelty seem justified. The most obvious example has been racism, the assumption that not to be white is to be deficient and inferior, to lack something crucial to full citizenship or even humanity. Then we learned about sexism, the assumption that those who are not male are incapable of participation in public life and exercise of responsibility. Then it was ableism, the assumption that those who are differently abled are "defective" and must be isolated and controlled. And there is speciesism, the assumption that all things exist to serve the needs or whims of the human race, that their very being is dispensable. In all these ways, difference is transmuted into inferiority, which then seems to be a reason to be deprived of dignity or regard.

Even when there is real deprivation, it may be difficult to perceive it and gauge its importance. The relative deprivation theory developed by social psychologists is Augustinian through and through.[11] People can be poor but not know what to call it; there is not a housing problem until people are told about it. Consciousness is important to the dynamics of human life. Revolutions are most likely to occur in times of rising expectations, when poverty and oppression do not seem hopeless and irremediable, or when the dynamics of change are breaking up customary inequalities and people begin to suspect that they have a right to more. When people feel unhappy about their condition, they feel it not "absolutely" but by comparison with what *other persons* have (their "comparative reference group") or with what *they themselves* might have (their "normative reference system"). Moralists can caution them against envy, and philosophers can wax eloquent about *ressentiment* and the differences between noble souls and their valets; but politicians had better attend to the hopes that circulate in a society, the comparisons that are made, the sense that people have of where they are in relation to other groups and to others in their own group, and their efforts to correct the situation on their own or in concert with others.

Of course relative deprivation is a matter of perception and attitude. Expectations may *exceed* the realistic potentialities for change; they may also *fall short* of them. Disparities of income, wealth, and power are greater in the United States than in most of the world's democracies. And yet most U.S. citizens characterize themselves as "middle class" and tend to identify more readily with the rich and powerful than with the weak. There are many explanations: the frontier and other symbols of unlimited possibilities; a level of security sufficient to make people fear losing what they have more than they desire gaining what they do not have; or the pervasive influence of the Protestant ethic, which guarantees that poverty will be interpreted as failure and wealth will be justifiable as long as it appears to have been gained through exertion in the race of life.

Under such circumstances, feelings of relative deprivation can take remarkable forms. White males may feel victimized by civil rights and affirmative action for women and minorities, or by provision of public services to immigrants. Those who hold conventional views of marriage and the family may think it is cultural outrage to call for equal treatment of gays and lesbians. Those who have been specially favored will always feel deprived when their privileges are questioned or diminished; it is the obverse of the deprivation felt by the less advantaged. Social change is initiated by one sense of deprivation, and its fulfillment gives rise to another. The only way to transcend these perspectival differences and the selfishness they encourage is to think in terms of justice, which means equitable procedures, equitable treatment, and equitable access to essential resources. It is dangerous to base moral judgments either on external characteristics or on inward feelings without self-critical reflection.

These modern-day examples suggest the continued relevance of Augustine's interest in thinking through the problem of evil in a comprehensive way, analyzing it as privation, reflecting on all possible cases, and tracing the role of defect and privation both in the origin of evil actions and in our perception of what is evil in our own situation.

Questions for Reflection

1. What in our experience leads us to take a "Manichaean" view of good and evil?

2. Do you think that the privation theory takes evil seriously enough? If not, what is the alternative?

3. How are we to judge the difference between real and perceived deficiency and privation?

CHAPTER FOUR

TIME AND CREATION: INTERPRETING GENESIS

The first chapters of Genesis were important to early Christians, not just because they told about beginnings, but because the perspective of Genesis seemed similar to that of Plato in his *Timaeus*. The convergences seemed to make both traditions more credible.

Ancient readers recognized that there are two creation narratives in Genesis. The older one, called the Yahwist by modern scholars, starts at Gen 2:5 and tells of the molding of the man from the soil. The younger narrative, called the Priestly, reaches from 1:1 to 2:4. To Philo and early Christian interpreters, this initial narrative looked like a description of the ideal world by which the material world is formed. They noticed, for example, that "image of God" comes prior to "male and female," and thus it might refer to the creation of the soul before it becomes embodied and sexually differentiated. Gregory of Nyssa even proposed a four-stage creation: God first intends to create human beings in God's own image, but then, foreseeing their fall into an earthly condition, decides also to create them male and female; Adam is formed from the earth, and Eve is taken from his side, but then, after they actually sin, they are clothed with "tunics of skin" (Gen 3:21), that is, mortality and the mind of the flesh, the medium in which human history is played out.

Time

Augustine paid repeated attention to the creation narrative in Gen 1.[1] We shall come in a moment to the details of his interpretation. But the opening words, "In the beginning," sent him into a chain of preliminary reflections filling the entire Book XI of the *Confessions*. He was always a careful thinker, wrestling with perplexities and demanding that we reflect along with him.

Tertullian had asked what God was doing before making heaven and earth, and his mocking answer was, "Creating a hell for people who ask such questions." Augustine rebukes this attitude, saying that it is a serious and profound question that should be respected and pondered carefully.

He argues that time does not exist by itself, because it is dependent on changes in finite things; before those things existed there could be no time. He could have acknowledged that we are able to think about tens of thousands or millions of years in the past (billions were well beyond his imagination), but the chronologies in the Bible (the Septuagint and its Latin translations) put creation at around 5000 B.C.E., so those millions of years have status only as a mathematical projection, not as any kind of reality.

Then Augustine, always the philosopher, moves to another question: "What is time? I know what it is until someone asks me, and then I find that I do not know."[2] It is the difference between having intuitions and being able to verbalize them. So he tries to answer his own question.

Time is grounded in the changes of finite things. But events occur and then perish. What is future is not yet, what is past is no longer; only the fleeting present is real. This is a pointillistic view of the world, very similar to what Alfred North Whitehead more recently said about the world as a plurality of occasions independent of each other but also influencing each other in an ongoing web of interactions.

Since events are pointillistic, the heart of Augustine's inquiry is, first, how we can *be aware of* time and, second, how we can *measure* the passage of time. This is why he turns to the mind, and what he finds is a "distention of the mind," a stretching of awareness that bridges future, present, and past; attention endures, and that is how we are able to know and measure the passage of time. This does not mean that time is "merely mental"; change really occurs. But mental acts outrun and outlast physical events. Awareness and measurement begin in the mind. Today measurement is helped by mechanical or electronic devices; before these existed, it had to be done with heartbeats, dance, or poetic rhythms.

A rhetorician like Augustine knew that making a speech requires anticipation of what will be said, awareness of what is being said, and memory of what has been said. Music gets its character through experienced tones, remembered patterns, and tensions and expectations that are constantly being amended or enriched or challenged. Beethoven and Brahms experimented with ambiguous chords that aroused uncertainty; Wagner and Richard Strauss created even greater suspense with their constantly changing harmonies. The "philosophy of action" looks at what is involved in starting a project and carrying it through; obviously an action of this kind involves many subacts that must be performed in the proper sequence, requiring sustained attention. The other side of it, of course, is that a lapse of attention on the part of the speaker or hearer or agent can break the flow. Attention deficit disorder and Alzheimer's disease involve a drastic loss of connected attention; but all of us have experienced it much too frequently.

The same is true of space, by the way. The world is not "in" the "box" of space that we think we perceive; the box of space is the structure of expectations that we have developed on the basis of experience, seeing how events both interact and stand apart from each other. Augustine held a relativistic view of space: if everything were to be half or double its size, we would not know it (of course the modern physicist would point out that all the natural forces would then be different, making any change of size very noticeable indeed; but strictly in terms of geometry, his point is valid.) And yet Augustine was not fully consistent. He rejected the view that the earth is round and there might be people standing upside down on the other side. For him down is down. When the sun, planets, and stars set, they do not go under the earth; they travel to other regions of an arched earth, and their orbits would probably have to be not circular but bent, warped.[3] Other people, even in the early Middle Ages, thought more carefully about this problem of the "antipodes" and gave a different answer, and Augustine became a symbol of resistance to scientific inquiry.

Awareness of time, whenever it occurs, involves anticipation and recollection. But these often gain intensely personal overtones as well. We have hopes and fears about the future. We try to shape the future by saving or burning our papers, writing wills, inscribing plaques, and endowing institutions. Augustine suggested that the reason some of the angels fell is that they were uncertain about their destiny, and anxiety led to self-concern.[4] There is pathos in the fact that the past is lost and cannot be reenacted; because it is our own past, nostalgia can make us compulsive hoarders. We may have deep regret, perhaps obsessively, about things that we did and cannot take back.

Thus the distention of the mind, while it is essential to awareness and measurement of time, can also mean dispersion, distraction, and frustration. In one famous passage, Augustine says:

> I have been spilled and scattered among times whose order I do not know; my thoughts, the bowels of my soul, are torn apart. . . . And so it will be until all together I can flow into you, refined and melted by the power of your love. Then I shall be stable and firm in your truth.[5]

That is also how he describes the "ecstasy in Ostia,"[6] when he and Monica were talking about heavenly rest, rising above changeable things. If these other things were to become silent, he suggests, then the "moment of undivided understanding" that they experienced would become their permanent state, with no fond regrets about the past or anxious anticipation of what is still to come. Paul Tillich liked to say that eternal life is not a quantity but a quality of life.

Finite minds are intrinsically temporal, but the effects of temporality can be overcome when they adhere to God and are free of disruption. The good angels enjoy the presence of God while they act temporally, administering the world in accordance with God's purposes (in fact, Augustine thought that, since God is not an agent in time and space, it is the angels who carry out providence). Something like this would have been possible for human life, too, but it is a lost possibility, approximated only in faith, hope, and love in the midst of many distractions and disruptions.

Time and the future are also involved in Augustine's understanding of human fulfillment, what we hope and strive for. As we have seen (ch. 2), classical culture understood fulfillment in terms of happiness; and when it asked what can give happiness, it generally concluded that it is found only in contemplating God, for the object is not used up in the process of enjoyment and there is no rivalry, since all can share in the same fulfillment. It is the one situation that is free of frustration or anxiety.

Creation

Now we are ready to move through Gen 1 and part of 2, following the sequence of the verses. Augustine has an interesting literal interpretation of Genesis. It might not have occurred to any of us, but it takes the text seriously in all its details. (Note that *literal* can mean reading some words as metaphors. Augustine approaches Genesis as though it were a "metaphysical poem" by John Donne or by Edward Taylor in colonial Massachusetts, who wrote of God blowing the bellows of the furnace and bowling the sun into space. God must be at least this imaginative.)[7] This interpretation is not totally new with Augustine; in its major outlines it comes from Origen and, farther back, from Philo of Alexandria. If you are given grief by friends who insist on a literal interpretation of Scripture, try this one out on them! It is at the same time a marvelous example of bringing the Bible into encounter with the science and philosophy of the ancient world.

The Beginning is the divine Word, who begins everything by speaking (cf. John 1:1, "In the beginning was the Word"). God creates the heaven (the spiritual creation) and the earth (corporeal matter). The earth (corporeal matter) is empty and formless; and there is darkness on the face of the deep. (This deep is the spiritual creation, which is, to be sure, "deep" but is also intrinsically restless, changeable, formless.)

Matter is that which is other than God, different from God; there could be no world *distinct* from God if it were not *different* from God. God is what Hegel called "good infinity," perfectly coherent; matter is "bad infinity," totally dispersive. Matter, Augustine says, is always "other" and "otherwise," even from itself. It is "something" but "next to nothing," not yet anything definite.

Augustine even speaks of "spiritual matter" in characterizing the angels. This is something he learned from Plotinus, who learned it from Aristotle. The point is that matter, whether corporeal or spiritual, is unstable and dispersive, awaiting formation, either through natural form or through knowledge (it was Aristotle who taught us to speak of knowledge as "information"). Both free choice and chaotic matter have a stark emptiness about them; when we look into this abyss, we see that it could become anything, or remain "no thing," or become what it *should not* be; it is the locus of monsters in the closet and demons inside ourselves. Formless depths haunt the world, and we can see why early Christian thinkers, when they reflected on creation, emphasized not the origin of matter but its formation. God is the one who "con-tains" (that is, holds together) a world that by itself tends toward dispersion and chaos.

Then God says (in and through the divine Word), "Let there be light." This is not the big bang but another kind of light, when no sun or stars yet existed—a call to the spiritual creation, the angels. Angels and demons were important in the Jewish tradition, and even more among the Greeks: to them the regular orbits of the heavenly bodies seemed to be proof that they were moved by intelligent beings. It was surprising that the Bible made no mention of their creation, so people looked for it and this passage was a likely candidate. "Let there be light" is an invitation to the spiritual creation, which in itself is darkness and fluidity, to turn toward the divine Light, become light in a reflected way, and gain stability by adhering to God. Just as they had no right to be created with unformed life, they had no right to receive light and gain stability; both result from divine generosity.[8]

"And there was evening and morning, one day." In Augustine's culture, a day began in the morning and ended in the evening. He may not even have known that the Hebrew day started at sunset; in any case, he thought that this unusual sequence must be a hint of a different meaning. Furthermore, the text says "one day," not "first day." This one day, Augustine thinks, must be the light of the angels as they turn toward God, with "evening knowledge" of themselves and "morning knowledge" as they refer that knowledge to the praise of God. Night never falls; both evening and morning are twilight. Along with these two kinds of knowledge, the angels also have a direct knowledge of God, called "noonday knowledge"; through it they know *even themselves* better in God than in themselves.

The rest of the days are the "ordered knowledge" of the angels as they consider the different realms of the created world. Augustine thought that matter was both created and formed at the first moment, just as, when we speak, we simultaneously produce sound and shape it into words. This was how he avoided any thought that God acts "in time" or interacts with the world. Although the world was formed all at once, at the first moment, there are these different realms that are surveyed by the angels, considering one cross section of creation and then another. In each iteration, the angels understand through illumination by the divine Word; the Spirit is also mentioned in God's seeing in each realm that creation is "good."

In describing how everything was formed at the first moment, Augustine drew upon the Stoic theory of "seminal reasons," much like what we call the "genetic code," ready to form growing organisms under the appropriate conditions; this is how living things can be self-ordering. He did not think that the world was created ready-made; organisms started not fully grown but in their seeds, their genetic material, and their full potential was not yet manifested. Augustine's theory was sometimes used in the nineteenth century to justify the new theory of evolution, and it may have helped soften up people's thinking; but it is really a theory of the permanence of species, based on the supposition that all matter was formed in the first moment of time. Although Augustine saw all sorts of hidden potentialities in the world, his theory does not take into account the rapid changes in the genetic code, especially in bacteria and viruses, that cause so much trouble for medical practice, or the recombination of genes, which has therapeutic possibilities.

Then God says, "Let us make humanity *to* our image and likeness"—or rather Image and Likeness, since most ancients thought that this must be the divine Word, God's full and undistorted image or self-representation, a perfect likeness of the Father. Humanity is merely created *to* God's Image. The meaning in the Greek and then the Latin translations is clearly "in accordance with" or "to" rather than "in" (the Hebrew prepositions can be taken either way). There were two possible interpretations. It could mean that human life images God only when it is actually turned toward God; when it falls away it loses the image because it no longer reflects God. Or it could mean that the human mind or soul *is* the image, a lesser imitation of God; the image in this sense cannot be lost, only distorted or covered over. Augustine first took the former view, then the latter, developing it most fully in his work *On the Trinity*. A major reason he gave for the change is that the human mind is the image of God, not merely of the Word.

Either way, for Augustine *image of God* refers to the human mind or spirit, in which male and female are equal. Then the text goes on to say, "male and female God created them," with their bodily differences. Following the assumptions of his age, Augustine thought that the female is inferior to the male, and that this is the one kind of inequality that comes from the "order of nature" and not from sin; because of this bodily inferiority, woman also symbolizes the "lower" and more vulnerable functions of the mind. Feminist scholars have come to mixed judgments about Augustine's view of women. Some emphasize that he affirmed the spiritual equality of women, against other interpreters who said that "image of God" refers only to males (this seemed to be implied by 1 Cor 3:18; 4:4-6; and 11:7). Others are more concerned about his influence in shaping Western Christian thought, both Catholic and Protestant; and it is true that he encouraged fear, shame, and guilt about sexuality. Taking the male point of view, he associated temptation with Eve, who symbolizes the affections, although he held Adam, who symbolizes the mind and is thus the decision-maker, to bear the chief responsibility for sin. His last word, however, is that in faith there is "no male and female" (Gal 3:28, reversing Gen 1:27), for all are one in Christ; and in the resurrection there is neither marrying nor giving in marriage, for they are like angels (Matt 22:30; Luke 20:35-36). His legacy to the West in this as in other ways is a complex one.

The bridge from the first to the second creation narrative mentions, once again, "the day" when God "made heaven and earth." Then the new narrative speaks of "every green thing of the field *before it was upon the earth*, and all the grass of the field *before it sprang up*" (Gen 2:5). This is idiomatic Hebrew usage, but it was translated literally, and Augustine interpreted it to mean that all living things are created together and at once, at the beginning of time, in their "seminal reasons."

God forms the man from earth and breathes life, the soul, into him. Then God sees that "it is not good that the man should be alone" and decides to "make for him a suitable helper." This, Augustine thinks, is not for the sake of companionship (for that, another man would have been more appropriate), but for reproduction. So God takes the woman from the man's side and breathes life into her.

At this point we should note that Augustine throughout his career was bothered by the question of how the soul gets into the body. He listed four different answers: nature (propagation from one generation to the next), God (creation of souls one by one), necessity (God's sending the soul into this body and destiny), or will (the soul's spontaneous movement toward it).[9] While he held open the first two possibilities, he tilted toward the last two. Because of his emphasis that all things were made at once and all together, he thought it likely that all human souls were created at the first moment but remain dormant until each is ready to be embodied in "its own" life.

Thus the world is created and formed at the first moment, ready to develop into living organisms that interact in many ways. Now we come to what happens *after* creation.

We who are born into the world as it now exists can easily imagine a better situation for human life than what we experience. The Eden narrative in Gen 2–3, being placed first, came to be used as what scholars call an etiological narrative, an attempt to explain the present by looking to origins. The sin of Adam and Eve results in pain in childbearing (Gen 3:16), laboring in the sweat of one's brow (Gen 3:19), and death itself, which is mentioned in God's threat at the very beginning (Gen 3:3) and is fulfilled in humanity's returning to the ground from which it was molded (Gen 3:19). This is the aspect emphasized in Paul (especially in Rom 5 and 1 Cor 15) and in later doctrine influenced by him.

The situation might be even more drastic. In the ancient world there were various expressions of cosmic insecurity. (Think of our anxieties today about global warming, nuclear winter, and killer asteroids—to say nothing of more familiar hurricanes, earthquakes, and tsunamis.) Gnosticism saw the current state of humanity as the result of a fall from the divine realm or, in the case of Manichaeism and similar movements, an imprisonment of good by evil. Some Platonists in the second century picked up Plato's suggestion that the World Soul is fallible, able to turn toward evil and needing to be stabilized by higher divine principles. Origen thought that a primordial fall of finite spirits led God to create a series of worlds for pedagogical purposes, to lead them back home.

Augustine rejected all such notions; for him God had no other reason for creating the world than to make it "very good" (Gen 1:31). But he did take seriously the riskiness of the world God has created; to say that it is "very good" must mean that it has maximum diversity, interaction, and intensity. This reaches all the way to the top of the cosmic hierarchy. If there had been no spirits in the highest levels of the cosmos who were able, if they fell, to shake it to its foundations, neither would there have been the good angels who maintain stability in the cosmos.[10]

Most early Christian thinkers supposed that human beings, like the rebel angels, must have "fallen" from a better state. But that was not the only possible approach. Augustine for a number of years held open the possibility that the discomforts of human life are natural, willed by God as a pedagogical challenge to grow and seek divine assistance.[11] Even his interpretation of the angels suggests this, since they were created in a state of fluidity but were simultaneously invited to turn toward God (according to John 8:44, Satan "never stood in the truth"). Later Augustine would reject this possibility on the principle that it is inappropriate for created spirits to make themselves better than God made them, and through their own free response at that.[12] Some of the Pelagians continued to assert that human life in its present state is how God created it at the beginning. But the later Augustine thought it improper to make the Creator responsible for human ills, and he mocked "the Paradise of the Pelagians" in which there would be lust, morning sickness, miscarriages and deformities, labor pains, suffering, and bereavement.[13] The evils that are *suffered* must be the result of evils that have been *done*.

Through all these shifts of nuance, Augustine always appreciated what Philo, Plotinus, and he himself called the "middleness" of human life: it is "in the middle" between body and spirit, higher and lower values, past and future. The human soul is changeable, and yet it has a vast range of awareness, such that it can be attracted to many things or be distracted from one thing by another or imagine new possibilities for itself.

The main line of theological discussion in the early church, different from both Origen and the Gnostics, began with Irenaeus around the year 180. He thought of human life as "situated freedom"—situated within the garden of Eden in each other's presence and confronted by the tempting serpent too. It is called to growth, education, improvement within this world. "First the animate, then the spiritual," says Paul (1 Cor 15:46). In keeping with this principle of education and progress, Irenaeus's most fascinating suggestion is that Adam and Eve were created neither mortal nor immortal but with the capacity for either: disobedience would lead to death; obedience would enable them to eat from the tree of life. He was using Aristotle's "three-valued logic": a proposition is either true, or false, or (the third) not yet decided. For Irenaeus the world is, as Keats put it, not a "vale of tears" but a "vale of soul-making."[14]

On this view, ever since Adam and Eve sinned (probably through a combination of naiveté and self-concern, although Satan, tempting through the serpent, bore the main responsibility), the history of the human race has been shaped by three factors, all acting simultaneously: human nature, which is incomplete at its beginning and is invited to develop in the right direction; sin, moral evil, which has occurred from the very beginning and distorts human development, individually and socially; and redeeming grace, which has always been at work. From the late second century on, it was assumed that Adam and Eve received salvation, and Augustine agreed. The contrast between sin and salvation continues in Cain and Abel and all the way through the biblical narrative. Even those who receive the promises of God must continue to struggle, and peace is to be found only after death, under quite different conditions.

This sober perspective on the human situation was shared by most Christian thinkers. Augustine's originality consists in enhancing its drama, radicalizing both sin and grace.

Questions for Reflection

1. Augustine in reading Gen 1 tries to be faithful to the text. And yet he also reads it as an expression of, and answer to, some of our most profound and puzzling experiences. What do you think of this as an approach to biblical interpretation?

2. Augustine and his age had various scenarios about the origin of the human situation as it is today. What parallels to this kind of reflection do you hear today? How can we go about evaluating them? (Please note that these issues will also come up in the next section, with new complications.)

CHAPTER FIVE

ORIGINAL SIN AND PREDESTINATION: THREATS TO FREEDOM?

Augustine is both praised and blamed for these doctrines, certainly major themes in Western religion. Were there deep psychological reasons for his championing them? Perhaps there were, for he had earlier been attracted to Manichaeism with its gloomy picture of the human situation. In later years, Pelagius and his followers were able to quote Augustine against Augustine, citing his early anti-Manichaean writings and charging that he had reverted to their position with his new emphasis on original sin and the bondage of the will (Julian of Eclanum routinely referred to him as "the Manichaean"). On the other hand, it could mean quite simply that he took evil and weakness seriously and examined first one answer and then another; his personality was not primarily a gloomy one. Furthermore, he did not invent these doctrines. In the case of original sin, it was already tradition; but he did defend it in an articulate way. In the case of predestination, he came to be convinced, against his will, that it was what Paul taught. What is most important is that he refused to evade two of the most difficult issues in the Christian tradition but rather wrestled with them, exploring the deepest mysteries of evil, bondage, and deliverance.

Original Sin

Original sin was *one* widespread tradition in the early church, especially in North Africa. Infant baptism probably was not practiced in the earliest church. But by about 200 there is evidence of infants being baptized, especially if they were near death. This was pastoral in motivation, something to do for consolation in a difficult situation. Once the practice arose, it had to be justified. In the West it was explained by suggesting that there is something wrong about the infant: mortality, disordered affections, perhaps even sin and guilt that are the consequence of the sins of earlier generations, all the way back to Adam and Eve. The East had a different explanation for infant baptism, as a positive initiation into the family of God; and this, of course, is the tone of baptismal rituals today.

The church believed that baptism is necessary for salvation; for this reason it allowed lay persons, including women, to baptize in the event of an emergency. This, by the way, reinforced Augustine's belief in predestination. If an infant dies unbaptized, despite all the efforts of midwives and parents and clergy, it must be because the infant was not predestined, and the implication is that they should not blame themselves too much. At the other end of life, there were cases like the man who had lived virtuously but in old age took up a dissolute life. For Augustine predestination functioned as a theory to *explain what actually happens*, not to go against appearances.

Just the opposite would happen during the Reformation. The Calvinist or Reformed churches pointed out that Paul had forbidden women to speak in church or to exercise any office, even baptism. (This, of course, is not a part of their heritage that these churches emphasize today; they officially decided to ordain women during the twentieth century, and now they are proud of their progress on that point.) If women are forbidden to baptize, then baptism *cannot* be necessary for salvation, and elect infants are saved without it. Predestination may work *independently of* the sacraments of the church, especially for the children of believers (there was much attention to continuity from one generation to the next, interpreted with the biblical language of covenant). These are two logically consistent arguments, dealing with an emotionally loaded pastoral issue, with opposing conclusions that depend on the initial premises.

Scholars have resituated the Pelagian controversy in important ways. It began in Rome, where three quite different currents of thought converged: the African, with its nascent doctrine of original sin; the Origenist, with its belief in preexistence and reincarnation; and the Antiochene, which sought a clear alternative to both of these.[1] The question "how the soul gets into the body," which we have already discussed (ch. 4), was part of the debate; but the focal issue was whether, and how, Adam's sin affected his descendants: was it through *propagation* or merely through *imitation*?

Resistance to notions of "earlier sin" (whether Adam's or the preexistent soul's) was especially strong in Antioch, and it was brought to Rome around 400 by Rufinus the Syrian. He was not an insignificant figure; he came from Jerome's monastery in Bethlehem and was the chief reviser of the New Testament in the so-called Vulgate translation. Original sin seemed fatalistic in the linkage it made between generations; Origen's teaching seemed no better, for he ascribed the current situation of the soul to its earlier life. The alternative was that death is natural, punishments are only for individual sins, and infants do not die because of Adam's sin.

This is the position taken by Rufinus the Syrian and then Caelestius, both of them in Rome but representing a way of thinking widespread in the East. The two of them came to be linked with Pelagius, whose special concern was a slightly different one, not *mortality* but *freedom of choice*. What we know as Pelagianism was a combination of these two currents of thought, one stressing that *punishment is only for individual sins*, the other that *sinful acts cannot affect human nature*. It is not mere jesting to ask whether Pelagius was a Pelagian. He consistently refused to answer the question whether mortality was natural or the result of sin. To Augustine this was proof of his deviousness. But in fact all the condemnations of Pelagianism outside North Africa had to do with positions characteristic of Caelestius, only secondarily with those of Pelagius.[2]

Augustine wrote several times in Book X of the *Confessions*, "If you give what you command, then command what you wish."[3] In other words, we can obey God's will, but only through God's help. It was not his own idea. He based it on a passage in the Apocrypha, "No one can be continent unless God gives it" (Wis 8:21).[4] When Pelagius heard it read in the presence of an unnamed bishop in Italy around 405, he burst out in protest. This is probably when he wrote his book *On Nature*; during the next decade he would write another one with the assertive title *For Free Choice*. Human nature, he insisted, has a permanent capability for sinlessness. He acknowledged that people sin. But wrong choice, he asserted, cannot alter human nature. In contrast to Augustine, who was aware of the complex dynamics of the affections and the relational character of the self, Pelagius asserted that the "good of nature," freedom of choice, persists; it is always there, and if it is rusted over it can be burnished by the file of the law, the hammer of Christ's example and teaching, and the fire of the Spirit.[5] His was a theory of the "strong self" in both nature and will; he matched it with demands for purity that made no room for compromise, rejecting, for example, the nascent doctrine of purgatory.

This is the prehistory of the Pelagian controversy. It broke into the open in 411, when Caelestius was denied ordination in Carthage (Augustine had no role in this event; the prosecutor was Paulinus of Milan). For a few years there was relatively polite theological maneuvering. The next formal proceedings were in Palestine in 415. Orosius of Braga, a Spaniard, brought charges against Pelagius at a local synod; then Jerome coined the term *Pelagianism* in order to prosecute Pelagius at the regional council of Diospolis. They failed, avoiding defeat by asking that the matter be referred to Rome as a Western issue.

Augustine and his allies now risked confrontation not only with the East but possibly with Rome as well, jeopardizing the unity of the church that he had been touting so loudly during the Donatist controversy (see ch. 6). They seized the initiative and condemned the "new heresy" at two African councils in 416, whose actions were affirmed by Pope Innocent—but only partially, and in his own language. Pelagius and Caelestius appealed to a new pope, Zosimus, in 418, who declared their statements of faith unobjectionable and rebuked the accusers.

Were the Africans to go against the pope? After Innocent's response to the two African councils of 416, Augustine had said, in effect, "Rome has spoken; the matter is finished."[6] (That was not how Innocent had understood it; he was making only an interim judgment, probably hoping to reconcile the two camps.) Now Augustine's attitude toward Rome was less enthusiastic. He had rejected the Donatists' claim that only Africa possessed the truth. The same principle might apply to Rome too.[7] (It will be no surprise that the same thought was later enunciated by Catholic conciliarists and by the Reformers, questioning the assumption that the Roman church can speak for the entire church.)

Rome had only an appellate role, and the Africans kept the initiative, condemning the key doctrines of Pelagius and Caelestius in 418; direct confrontation with Rome was avoided by not mentioning them by name. The Africans were rescued by the imperial court in Ravenna, which condemned the Pelagians largely because of some writings from Sicily; their perfectionist approach to the Christian life led to a social critique that seemed dangerously revolutionary. Zosimus had to follow suit, sending a letter condemning them to the churches of the East in the summer of 418.

After this sudden reversal, a number of bishops in Italy and Illyria, led by Julian of Eclanum, called for examination of the issues in a general council, refusing in the meantime to submit; they compared themselves with the fourth-century bishops who opposed Arianism against the will of the emperor. They had a valid point. The condemnations had come first from the imperial court, and only then, under duress, from the pope. It was quite legitimate to call for a council where bishops could examine the doctrinal issues fully. Augustine, on his part, became the champion of uniformity, defending a new orthodoxy that was largely of his own making. The debate between Julian and Augustine went through three or four rounds, stretching from 420 to Augustine's death in 430.

People in many regions had trouble adjusting to the new orthodoxy, for there had been only three years' formal debate before reaching premature closure. In the coming decades even Augustine's followers were to mitigate his assertions about original sin and predestination. Yet there were also some momentous changes of opinion. In 418, consolidating his gains in Rome, Augustine wrote a strongly predestinarian letter to the presbyter Sixtus,[8] praising him for having turned away from Pelagianism; Sixtus may be the Sicilian author of the socially radical tracts, and he is the same Sixtus who, as pope, refused to rehabilitate Julian in 439, once again because the question had already been decided.

In the end, each side had a partial victory. Medieval and modern attitudes about the natural vulnerability of human life are more in continuity with Rufinus and Caelestius than with Augustine; but the nonrelational view of human life advocated by Pelagius and Julian has found few sophisticated champions.

Augustine sees human life as relational or "situated" in several different ways. It is influenced by previous generations, all the way back to Adam and Eve. It is influenced by the flow of impressions that are always coming toward us from the world, from other people, and from the culture. When our own affections are aroused by these impressions, we become accustomed to them and they become "second nature"; this is the bondage of the will to its own disordered desires, such that sin becomes its own punishment. Being "situated" in these various ways does not destroy free choice, but it does shape it. Moral evil is "never without will," Augustine says,[9] but the range of willing can be limited, with freedom for sin but not for good (cf. Rom 6:15-23).

When Augustine thinks in terms of the bondage of the will and original sin, he suggests that Adam's progeny choose evil *inevitably* but still *on their own responsibility*; then they go on to perpetuate cultural attitudes and social institutions characterized by self-indulgence for some and deprivation for others. But all of this is discovered only retrospectively. By the time we come to full awareness, we are already guilty.

The philosopher Kant made the same point in the late eighteenth century, retrieving the doctrine of original sin and renaming it "radical evil." Goethe was so shocked that he said Kant had "soiled his philosopher's robe." But Kant was serious about it. Finite freedom when it is embodied, especially in the unsophisticated situation of the first human beings, will inevitably make the wrong choices, even before it knows what it is doing. Then it discovers, sooner or later, its own guilt.

There are analogous debates in our own time about institutions that perpetuate misery and inequality—"structural evil" is the generic name for them. We ourselves may not have had any direct role in creating them. Yet some of us benefit from the fruits of slavery or of having white skin or of being male or of living in the West. Perhaps that means we are "guilty." At the very least it means that we have a responsibility to try changing them and reduce our benefits from them.

Or consider the dispute over juvenile delinquents and adult offenders. There are some in our society who emphasize "individual responsibility," and they are very close to Pelagianism despite the fact that they are often evangelical Christians. The alternative is to acknowledge the many psychological, social, and cultural forces that may have shaped someone's character; but this in turn is easily satirized in songs like "Poor Wandering Ones" in *The Pirates of Penzance* or "Gee, Officer Krupke" in *West Side Story*. Augustine was consistent: in controversy with both the Donatists and the Pelagians he took an "understanding" view of human shortcomings. By contrast Pelagius was a hard-line moralist, insisting on personal responsibility because everyone is capable at every moment of choosing good or evil. If Pelagius had won, the West would have been far more moralistic and punitive than it has been with Augustine as its moral and spiritual guide.

Predestination

The topic of bondage of the will leads us to predestination. *Why is it* that some people are freed from this bondage and others not?

Predestination is not the first answer that comes to mind, since it seems to conflict with free choice; early Christian thinkers tried to avoid it, and Augustine did too, especially when he was opposing the Manichaeans' fatalism. His anti-Manichaean arguments influenced Pelagius and Julian, who then quoted them against the "later" Augustine. Looking back, he commented that he had argued "for free choice" (he purposely uses Pelagius's slogan) but grace prevailed.[10] This happened in 396 or 397, when he was convinced that grace has the initiating role. What persuaded him was Paul's statement that God chose Jacob and rejected Esau "before they were born, before they had done anything either good or bad" (Rom 9:11-13). In the *Confessions*, written immediately afterward, he told the story of his conversion, explaining it with the aid of this theory.

But then he was silent about predestination and prevenient grace for fourteen years, from 397 to 411, the beginning of the Pelagian controversy. Why? Perhaps he found no occasion to mention it. Perhaps he had yielded to the authority of Paul but then did not know what to do with it. Perhaps his discovery received a chilly reception, not only from Pelagius but from friends and influential church leaders.[11] What we do know is that during these years he was engaged in controversy with the Donatists (see ch. 6), asserting that the Holy Spirit dwells only within the Catholic Church and salvation is impossible outside it. He was insisting on grace and limiting the scope of salvation in another way, which he would later incorporate into his doctrine of predestination.

To understand Augustine's view of grace and predestination, we have to look at his theory of willing. It came originally from the Stoics, and by his time, modified in various ways, it was widespread among educated people of various philosophical camps.[12] The basic observation is that it is not in our power to determine what will "occur to us," either from external events or through the inward association of ideas. These impressions in turn arouse strong feelings and inclinations, drawing us this way and that. The outcome seems to be determined by what most delights us—or most terrifies us (Augustine liked to say that Satan is both lion and serpent, tempting through intimidation as well as desire); or, if they equally attract or repel us, then we waver between them. And of course our inclinations are reinforced by "custom," what we are accustomed to.

So there are three factors in willing. First comes the *suggestion*, which occurs to us either through the senses or through our own free association of ideas. This in turn arouses *inclinations*, especially of delight or fear or anger. But this is only a movement of the affections; there is no "act," either inward or outward, until *consent* is freely given in the center of the self. In consent we yield to or ratify some inclination that has already been aroused. Or perhaps we resist the inclination and consent to another. And even after consent has been given, there can remain a conflict of inclinations, resisting each other and even resisting what has been consented to. Jerome and Augustine, and later Luther and Calvin, emphasized that conflict is intensified in the elect who have responded to God's call but continue to feel temptations to the contrary. They are, we might say, always "in recovery." That struggle is what identifies them as saints. The apostles and martyrs feared suffering and death; but their loyalty to God was stronger.

How and why does one consent? When one is called "congruously," in a way suited to one's condition, one will respond to that call. This is why, in Book VIII of the *Confessions*, written soon after he came to believe in predestination, Augustine emphasizes that Antony, then he himself, then his friend Alypius were converted by hearing or reading passages from the Bible, exactly the passages that each needed to hear. In this narrative, his theory of "congruous calling" shapes his presentation of the events. The principle is that, if human willing is in bondage to its own misdirected affections, to such an extent that it cannot delight in or consent to or will the good, then it must be freed from that bondage by the divine call.

But is willing really freed if it merely passes from the inevitability of wrong delight to the inevitability of correct delight? This is a question that wracked post-Reformation Catholic theology, starting in the late sixteenth century and continuing well into the next. Both sides claimed Augustine, and both had some justification because he had made an important shift of emphasis around the year 418.

The Jesuits developed a subtle theory based on what Augustine was saying for many years up to 418. Grace, they said, acts not "physically," as one thing acts on another, but "morally," making an appeal through meanings and the affections; it "wins hearts and minds," using persuasion, not force. How? God knows how people *would respond* to various suggestions and ensures that the elect will receive exactly those suggestions that they would respond to. The human response does not happen *by necessity*; grace is not "intrinsically" irresistible. Yet it works *infallibly*, because God knows which suggestions will lead to a definite outcome. Persons are not made to act *unwillingly*; rather they are enabled to *become willing* to act in a new way.

This sounds very much like "behavior modification" in our own day. We have a sense of people's preferences, and we present various inducements that we know will be responded to; then we reinforce them. When it succeeds, we are likely to say, "I knew that is what you would do." It is popular wisdom that everyone has a price, and we are not just joking when we say, "I can withstand anything but temptation." The same applies to more positive invitations to generous behavior; another part of popular wisdom is that a child treated with love will learn to love.

The Jesuit theologians emphasized "congruous calling": a free act is evoked when God presents the appropriate inducements, and consent is the personal resolution of all the factors impinging upon oneself. The rival movement called Jansenism took another aspect of Augustine's thought and asserted it in direct opposition to the Jesuits. The Jansenists knew that Augustine in his later writings (from 418 on) emphasized the immediate influence of the Holy Spirit, infusing what he called a "victorious delight" in the good.[13] For them, this good delight acts as inevitably as the bad delight of the sinful will. They, like the Calvinists, stressed that grace is both efficacious and irresistible. The Jesuits, by contrast, stressed that grace is congruous, acting infallibly without being "intrinsically efficacious."

Both schools of thought were Augustinian. Their bitter disagreements came from failing to take seriously the full sequence of suggestion, delight, and consent. A free act is evoked both by the suggestions that occur to us and by the inclinations that are aroused, but there is not an act until there is consent in the center of the self, coming to terms, in one's own way, with these various influences. Even when both the suggestion *and* the delight come from God, their purpose is to free the will to act for the good. In the one passage where Augustine says that God's grace "cannot be resisted," he emphasizes that this does not happen through constraint, for God stirs the heart and "draws" it (cf. John 6:44) through its own affections.[14] Grace comes *to, into,* and *through* human freedom.

There were parallels in the Calvinist world. Jonathan Edwards, a pre-destinarian of the "moral influence" type, defined freedom as following the greatest apparent good or the strongest inclination. His followers, known as the Edwardsians, continued to explore the factors leading toward conversion. Their interest in the subtleties of human psychology was an important factor in shaping New England culture, even when it took radically different forms in Emerson and Thoreau, Hawthorne and Melville, Emily Dickinson and William James. What was kept was the psychological sensitivity of Edwardsianism; what was left behind was its limitation of salvation to the elect and its restriction of church membership to those who could give a convincing account of a saving experience. The Edwardsian tradition has remained alive and well, however, in revivalism, starting in the early nineteenth century with Charles Finney's "new measures"; it continues in the emotional appeals of the televangelists, which they would defend as moral influence or persuasion seeking an affirmative response.

Both bondage of the will and predestination are dramatic expressions of the view that the self is "situated." Many experiences seem to support these theories. And yet we may recoil at the view that God arbitrarily elects only some, letting the rest go to a well-deserved damnation.

Or do we really recoil at predestination that much? American culture has been shaped by Calvinist predestinarianism. The Puritans, somewhat like the Donatists, tried to ascertain who was saved and then gather a church of "visible saints." It was also the Puritans who perfected the "Protestant ethic," the work ethic, according to which self-discipline, thrift, and accumulation of wealth become signs of election, and the poor are those who lack discipline and are probably *not* elect. The "gospel of prosperity" is one contemporary expression of this tradition.

Marvin Olasky, father of the "compassionate conservatism" that was espoused by President Bush in his faith-based initiative, says that only the deserving poor should receive alms, dispensed not by social workers but by faith-based organizations using their own religious criteria to give alms or refuse them. (This, we might say, is behavior modification administered by the elect.) Olasky's political theology is stated most explicitly in *The Tragedy of American Compassion*, where he criticizes both social Darwinism (which considers some people to be intrinsically unfit and irreformable) and what he calls social universalism (the widespread assumption that all have "a right to eternal salvation and temporal prosperity") and proposes a third way that he calls, in one place, social Calvinism.[15] Here predestination leads away from a sense of *sharing* the human condition and toward claims of *special exemption* from it. The elect see themselves *against* the world, not *with* the world.

If we have qualms about predestination, what are the alternatives? The Christian tradition has softened Augustine's predestinarianism in several important ways.

One, verbalized by several councils in the 850s, emphasizes the *asymmetry* between salvation and damnation: salvation is through the grace of God, damnation is the result of human sin. Such an approach is compatible with both predestinarianism and Arminianism. Karl Barth gave this perspective a fresh twist by saying that the only appropriate response to the divine yes of grace is a human yes, but there is the "impossible possibility" of refusal, made possible, in fact, by the very offer of grace.

Another approach is to think of condemnation and salvation not as a zero-sum alternative, with "double issue" in either hell or heaven, but as *sequential*. In the early nineteenth century, Schleiermacher in Berlin and the Cumberland Presbyterians in Tennessee said that God's wisdom decrees that all people experience themselves first as sinners condemned by God, and only then as recipients of forgiving grace, so that they will be all the more grateful when they are offered salvation. William Sloane Coffin has put it this way: "we are one in sin, which is no mean bond, because it precludes separation through judgment"; then he goes on, "there is more mercy in God than sin in us."[16]

Questions for Reflection

1. What aspects of human experience suggest original sin or its modern versions? How would you go about trying to account for them?

2. In dealing with morality and the legal system, how should we balance an insistence on "personal responsibility" and sympathy with the many ways people are influenced by factors beyond their control?

3. How well does Augustine describe and analyze the relation between free will and grace? Would you agree with him that the Christian life comes entirely from grace and entirely from human freedom?

CHAPTER SIX

THE CHURCH AND THE SACRAMENTS: UNITY IN GRACE ACROSS SPACE AND TIME

Most of Augustine's writings were occasioned by intra-Christian disputes. The one that was closest to him, right at his front door, was with the Donatists. This North African movement claimed to have a purer church than the Catholic Church, not only in Africa but throughout the world. When Augustine became bishop of Hippo, Donatists were probably more numerous in that city than Catholics.

The movement grew out of the "Great Persecution" under Diocletian (303–313). Alleging that the bishop of Carthage had handed over copies of the sacred Scriptures to the authorities, a rival set of bishops was consecrated, and they associated themselves with the martyrs. (The facts have been in dispute from that day to this.) Their chief argument was that when a sinful clergy administered the sacraments they could not hand on what they themselves did not possess. The Donatists felt confident, furthermore, that they could identify the pure church; thus they are one of the first "sects" in the sociologists' meaning of the term. To Augustine they were like the Manichaeans in trying to make good and evil tangible and clearly differentiable.

The Donatists could claim Cyprian, the most venerable authority in the African tradition. In dealing with clergy who had "lapsed" during the earlier persecution under Decius (249–251), Cyprian decided that any baptisms and ordinations they performed were soiling, not sanctifying, the recipients. Stephen, the bishop of Rome, decided in the opposite way, arguing that the sacraments are Christ's, not the minister's.

Many people in North Africa were inclined, out of regional loyalty, to follow Cyprian and assume that the Roman church must be wrong. The issue was exacerbated by politics. The Donatists had appealed to Constantine in 316, but unsuccessfully, and under his son (from 346 to

361) they were severely repressed; thus it is not surprising that they developed the attitude, "What does the church have to do with the empire?" There was also an ethnic factor. W. H. C. Frend showed that areas of Donatist strength were those where Berber and Punic traditions were strongest; resentment against Roman overlords was readily translated into hostility toward the international church. Class warfare also played a role. Wandering bands of "circumcellions" used violence against Catholic travelers and forced landowners to destroy documents and labor at the treadmill; in their own minds they were "fighting the good fight" (1 Tim 6:12; 2 Tim 4:7). Augustine had the disadvantage of having been converted in Milan and being associated with cosmopolitan culture, the ruling classes, and the Roman Empire. No one could be more the outsider from the standpoint of many Christians in Africa. Their attitude was probably like that of Irish Catholics toward the Church of England, imposed on them by Henry VIII; to them it was the church of invaders, dispossessors, and landlords.

Augustine got the better of the argument, citing Cyprian against Cyprian. Even though Cyprian and his colleagues believed that their adversaries did not possess true baptism and were still under the power of sin, they received them without this baptism, preferring fellowship rather than separation from the unity of the church; Augustine notes, furthermore, that the worldwide church with which Cyprian was united not only endured but continued to gain converts throughout the world.[1] Cyprian was committed to maintaining "the unity of the Spirit in the bond of peace" (Eph 4:3 RSV), judging it to be more basic than details of practice and discipline. Augustine went one step farther, emphasizing this unity in love, rather than behavior, as the decisive factor in salvation.[2]

Although Augustine followed Cyprian in this respect, he adopted the Roman theory that the sacraments belong not to the bishop, not to the church, but to Christ. Just as the patriarchs begat children not only through their wives but through their handmaidens, so Christ can work through the Donatists' sacraments. Baptism, the "sacrament of faith" that is necessary for incorporation into Christ, is true baptism even when it is administered outside the unity of the church; it is not to be repeated when people rejoin the worldwide church, although hands are laid on them as a sign of repentance and reconciliation.

Augustine concedes this much to the Donatists. But they enjoy only the communion of the *sacraments*, not the communion of the *saints*. The Holy Spirit cannot dwell in those who are not within the unity of the worldwide church. In the language of later theology, the sacraments are *valid* when administered by the Donatists, but they are *efficacious* only within the unity of the *Catholica*, as it was called. If the Donatists claim that the church is holy because of the personal qualities of those who are in it, it only manifests their pride and provincialism. For Augustine the church is holy because the Holy Spirit dwells among those who humbly associate with other Christians, even those they consider inadequate. The Donatists may try to appropriate the heritage of the martyrs, and some of them still seek martyrdom; but Paul's saying applies to them: "If I give my body to be burned but do not have love, I gain nothing" (1 Cor 13:3).

Augustine agrees with Cyprian's statement that "outside the church there is no salvation" for the reason that the sacraments cannot take effect where the Holy Spirit does not dwell. The Donatists, like some of the later Puritans, tried to achieve a church "without spot or wrinkle" (Eph 5:27); they thought they could separate the wheat from the tares prior to the last judgment (cf. Matt 13:24-30). Augustine was less severe, following the principle that "charity covers a multitude of sins" (1 Pet 4:8). The Donatists employed spatial images of enclosure and exclusion, such as the ark (Gen 6:14) and the enclosed garden (Cant 4:12).[3] Augustine broadened his field of vision to the worldwide church and made an alternative distinction, between the church as it is here and now, mixed with sin and sinners, and the church as it will be in the future, without blemish.

If Augustine was harsh toward the Donatists, saying that they had the communion of the sacraments but not of the saints, he made the same point about many who belong to the Catholic Church. All who have been predestined are now, or will be, baptized and members of the one visible church; but not everyone in the visible church is among the elect. Augustine describes the visible church as at once the true and the false, the authentic and the adulterated church[4]; and this is the only church to be found on earth prior to entry into the heavenly Jerusalem. Like individual believers, it is engaged in constant struggle, even with itself. Nourished by the sacraments, it is "under grace," but it is not yet "in peace." These are points that Augustine learned from Tyconius, a Donatist who undermined the principles of his movement and was expelled in 380 but never joined the *Catholica*.[5]

For Augustine the sacraments are *signs*. They involve physical things and actions to be sure, but also words that make these things and actions into "visible words," conveying a spiritual power that outlasts the spoken words. But this spiritual power takes effect only within the unity of the one church. If the Eucharist is the sacrament of the body and blood of Christ, it is to be interpreted with the aid of the New Testament description of the church as the body of Christ (Rom 12:4-5; 1 Cor 12:12;

Eph 1:23, 2:15; Col 1:24, 3:11). The reality to which the sacramental signs refer is the unity of "the whole Christ," head and body; those who receive it in a worthy manner become one loaf, one body in Christ.[6]

When we look back at Augustine through the lens of the Reformation and its disputes, we find that his emphasis on the visible unity of the church is more like the Roman Catholic position, while his view of the eucharistic signs is more like the one held by Ratramnus in the ninth century, Berengar in the eleventh, and most Protestants. To be sure, he does say that the loaf and the cup become the body and blood of Christ—but in the sense that they become a "visible word." His clearest statement concerns baptism, but it applies to the Eucharist as well:

> The word comes to the elements and makes a sacrament, as a visible word.
> . . . Why does the water have such power that it touches the body and
> washes the heart, except that the word acts? Not because it is spoken,
> but because it is believed.[7]

Augustine's view of the Eucharist is probably close to that of contemporary Catholic theologians who speak of "transignification" rather than transubstantiation. Christ is spatially absent, sitting at the right hand of God. His absence is changed into presence with the aid of the visible signs, yes, but chiefly by faith; faith reaches out to him, and he comes to dwell in human hearts through faith (cf. Eph 3:17).[8]

Dialogue and reunion with the Donatist clergy was proposed by the Catholic bishops in 401 and initiated, under government pressure, in 403; there were individual conversions, which in turn drew physical retaliation from Donatists. Augustine at first trusted persuasion, then he supported punishment of violent acts. After an imperial edict of 405 required the Donatists to reunite with the Catholics, he hailed it, in large part because former Donatists said they were grateful for this external nudge toward the true church. Thus Augustine defended the coercion of the Donatists, citing Christ's directive, "Compel them to come in" (Luke 14:23). His famous dictum "Love and do as you will" was uttered in the context of the coercion of the Donatists: the means, he says, may look harsh, but you cannot go wrong if you are motivated by love.[9] (By our time we have learned that justice may be more difficult than love, for love without justice can lead to battered children and spouses and many kinds of manipulation of people "for their own good.")

The watershed event was a conference of the Catholic and Donatist bishops in 411, called by the imperial court and presided over by one of its officials. The professed purpose was reconciliation, not repression, and the Donatists' appeal to the court in 406 was used in 411 as an argument that they themselves had called for a conference of exactly this sort. Slowly they *were* reconciled, through a combination of pressure and leniency, over the next decade; but bishops often had to deal with recalcitrant members who remained loyal to Donatist traditions.

Augustine had much more to say about "the whole Christ" outside the Donatist controversy. For him this was a key to the unity of the Bible. He heard the Psalms as the voice of the whole Christ—head and body— sometimes repenting for sins and crying out for salvation; sometimes, as in the enthronement psalms, praising Christ as the exalted ruler; sometimes struggling with enemies, questioning the prosperity of the wicked, or mourning captivity in Babylon; sometimes speaking as the voice of Christ himself, who identifies with the members of his body and prefigures what they are to become through their own renewal and resurrection.

The notion of "the whole Christ" helped Augustine to interpret the entire biblical story. Especially in his work *Against Faustus the Manichee* he rescued the Old Testament for Christianity, showing how the two Testaments belong together. The rituals of ancient Israel, while different from the Christian sacraments, are signs of the same grace and the same faith. Ancient Israel believed in Christ as still to come; the church believes in Christ as having already come. What is latent in Israel becomes patent in the gospel of the church. The biblical narrative tells of sin, of course, but primarily of salvation, prefigured long before the incarnation; in one vivid passage Augustine says that the saints in Israel were already members of the whole Christ in process of birth, putting forth a hand and other parts of the body before the head emerged.[10]

What does this mean for Christian attitudes toward Jews? Augustine had some harsh things to say about the Jews of his own time, calling them disobedient and blind to the truths set forth in their own Bible; some features of his writings doubtless fueled prejudice against the Jews in medieval and Reformation times. Even in criticizing them, however, he gave the Jews a constructive role: they preserve the same Bible that the Christians use, proving that this Bible, with its foreshadowings of Christ, is not a Christian fabrication. But there was more beyond this left-handed compliment.

Augustine is the source of an affirmative view of the Jews that has always been one part of Western thinking. He saw positive significance in the ceremonies of the law of Moses as manifesting the same grace, the same faith, as that announced in the New Testament. The saints of ancient Israel, as we have seen, were part of the body of Christ, and, starting with the apostles, many Jews have been brought to Christ. In the spirit of Paul in Rom 10–11, Augustine warns Gentile believers not to exalt themselves, since the Jews are the only hereditary people of God, and even the Catholic Church is the mixed catch of fish (Matt 13:47-50) that contains some who will be rejected.

In an earlier section we saw how Augustine understood time and space as threatening dispersion and fragmentation. In thinking of the church as the body of Christ he found a unique kind of unity across worldly time, starting with Adam and Eve and Abel, and across worldly space, with a mission to the whole human race. In the proclamation the church makes to the whole world, and in the unity of love among Christians throughout that world, it bridges the many differences of culture, power, and status that threaten to divide people from one another.

Questions for Reflection

1. Cyprian and Augustine, in dealing with at least one major issue, made the dramatic statement that it is more important "to maintain the unity of the Spirit in the bond of peace" (Eph 4:3) than to insist on one's own doctrinal certitudes. How is this helpful in dealing with our own differences and disputes? Where, if anywhere, is the "breaking point"?

2. How helpful is Augustine's theory of the sacraments as "signs" for understanding what happens in Christian worship?

3. Augustine affirms that Israel and the church share the same grace and faith but with different signs and ceremonies. How might this help modern Jewish-Christian dialogue?

CHAPTER SEVEN

TRINITY AND INCARNATION: SHAPING DOCTRINE IN THE WEST

W hen Augustine entered the Catholic Church in 387, there was still controversy over both the Trinity and the incarnation in at least two ways. The doctrines themselves were contested, and even when a definite position was taken as a matter of *faith* there was still a need to *understand and conceptualize* these affirmations.

The Trinity

The councils of Nicaea (325) and Constantinople (381) had declared that the Son is "of the same essence" as the Father (as we shall see, the language of parent and offspring is more accurate). In Milan, however, the Arians, who said that the Son is "less than" the Father, had the support of the regent Justina—and of the Gothic mercenaries; the Catholic bishop Ambrose was engaged in constant controversy with them. After Augustine returned to Africa, Arianism may have been a "textbook heresy" for some years, but it once more became a living presence when Goths were stationed in Africa. He answered a "sermon of the Arians" in 419 and debated the Arian bishop Maximinus in 427 or 428.

Augustine's earliest explorations of the doctrine focused on manifestations of the Trinity in the finite world. He read that all things have their being "in God" (Acts 17:28) and that God is the one "from whom, through whom, and in whom" all things exist (Rom 11:36). The book of Wisdom, furthermore, said that God has ordered all things according to "measure, number, and weight" (Wis 11:20). Augustine suggested, therefore, that traces of the Trinity are seen in the structure of all finite beings: in matter, form, and movement or in being, truth, and goodness or in the division of philosophy into physics, logic, and ethics.

He was convinced that all human beings are "illuminated" by the divine Word (John 1:4; cf. Rom 1:20, 2:14-15), even when they do not respond. He saw evidence of this in the writings of the Platonists, writings that had the same lucid glow as the first chapter of John. This conviction remained the same through the forty-three years of his writing career.

He had more perplexities concerning the Holy Spirit. When he started a commentary on Romans he took a detour to discuss the first few verses and never went any further. He noticed that Paul mentioned God and Christ, then spoke of "grace and peace"; recognizing a problem, he reasoned that these words must refer to the Holy Spirit as the divine gift, a gift that is not inferior to the giver. Then he wondered about the unforgivable sin against the Holy Spirit (Matt 12:31-32) and decided that this must be despair over the grace of God or spurning the means of grace that are offered through the church and its sacraments—an error manifested in one way by the Pelagians and in another by the Donatists.[1]

Or again, he reflected on the statements that "love is from God" and "God is love" (1 John 4:7-8) and the warning that one who hates a brother or sister, who is seen, cannot love God, who is not seen (1 John 4:20-21). This must mean, he concluded, that when we experience our own act of love we experience the Holy Spirit.[2] That suggestion caused a major dispute among the medieval scholastics: does it mean that the Spirit *is* the human act of love? The answer that seemed most satisfactory was that, since the *act* is human, the *agent*, too, must be human rather than divine, but both the act and the capability to act are evoked by the indwelling of the Holy Spirit.[3]

Augustine's most sustained discussion was his work *On the Trinity*, which he began around 400 and finished around 420 (he commented, with some exaggeration, that he had started it as a youth and ended it as an old man). It is a major example of "faith seeking understanding."

In the first books he supports the Nicene doctrine with arguments from Scripture, both the Old and New Testaments. His rule of interpretation is that passages suggesting that the Son is less than the Father apply to his humanity, while those suggesting that he is equal to the Father apply to his divinity. In the process he had to attend to passages saying that the Word appeared to the patriarchs and to Moses. Earlier interpreters thought this implied that the Word was "less than" God. Augustine says that these theophanies were staged by the angels, created beings who act in space and time, though truly signifying the Word of God.

For many years Augustine was puzzled about how to deal with the *eternal* Trinity, the Trinity *within* God. Neither scripture nor the creed offered much help. He got his answer from the so-called Cappadocians, especially Gregory Nazianzen, writing in the East only a few decades earlier; they have come to be called "doctors" or "teachers" of the church because they clarified doctrine in a way that councils could not.

Their crucial insight was that the words *Father* and *Son* are used not because God is sexual or grows like a human embryo, but solely because these are relational terms: one is a parent only by having an offspring, and vice versa. Thus they emphasize the "relations" of begetting, begotten, and proceeding, and these alone differentiate the three persons; the one divine essence is identical in all three persons and is fully present in each. Augustine's rule of thumb is that what is said "relatively" refers to the three persons; what is said "simply" refers to the divine essence.

Following up on this insight, Augustine understood the Trinity on analogy with the human mind, which the Bible calls the image of God. The mind, while remaining one, relates to itself in three ways: memory (immediate self-awareness), understanding (fully explicit self-concept), and will (self-love or self-affirmation). In making this comparison Augustine took care to emphasize the difference between human and divine mind. The former is full of unactualized potentialities, and these may be realized through erroneous self-concepts and misdirected affections; it is only in looking to God that one can set one's own knowledge and love in the right perspective. In God, by contrast, there are no unactualized potentialities; God's characteristics are complete, needing no supplementing. God does not *become* wise or good through the trinitarian relations; because God is already wise and good by nature, this perfection *overflows* or *unfolds* in the trinitarian relations. Here Augustine disagrees with several influential thinkers: Plotinus, for whom the three divine principles are hierarchical, each of them being perfected by turning toward the one above it; Porphyry and Marius Victorinus, who had a more "horizontal" Trinity, but one that is actualized by seeking and returning to itself; and Hegel, for whom God becomes fully actualized through the world process and human culture.

Augustine tried to state the doctrine of the Trinity as precisely as possible, and some of his formulations found their way into the so-called Athanasian Creed (it does not come from Athanasius but was written in southern Gaul around 525). It became a standard of orthodoxy in the West, far more exact than the Nicene Creed. Some of its language clearly comes from Augustine, as when it says,

> Thus the Father is God, the Son God, the Holy Spirit God, yet not three Gods but one God. Thus the Father is Lord, the Son Lord, the Holy Spirit Lord, yet not three Lords but one Lord.[4]

In formulations like these Augustine thought that he was moving beyond mere faith to understanding, a clear conceptualization of the truth. And yet he did not suppose that he was saying the final word. In the last books of *On the Trinity* he keeps calling for growth in faith and understanding.

It is better to keep on seeking, he says, than to presume that one has found; better yet, God is still to be sought even after being found.

Augustine gave definitive formulation to the doctrine of the Trinity in the West. He also caused a new dispute. The Nicene Creed affirmed that the Spirit proceeds from the Father (John 15:26). But Augustine thought that the Spirit proceeds from the Father *and the Son* (*Filioque* in Latin). This expression was used in the Athanasian Creed, from which it was transferred into the Western version of the Nicene Creed, although it had never been agreed on by a council of the whole church. The *Filioque* has been a major point of controversy between East and West until today. When Catholic and Anglican bishops say the creed with bishops from the Eastern churches, they now omit this phrase as a gesture of goodwill.

At a practical level, the *Filioque* has some important consequences, for it seems to narrow the scope of revelation and salvation. If the Spirit comes only with or through the Word, this seems to imply that the Spirit is "tied to" or "controlled by" the Word, which in mundane terms means scripture, the sacraments, and the church and its ministries. Thomas Aquinas said that the Greeks' denial of the Spirit's procession from the Son is like their denial of the primacy of the pope, the vicar of Christ, over the universal church: the church is kept subject to Christ by both the Spirit and the pope. In the Reformation churches, the *Filioque* was applied to slightly different effect. Against the "Spirituals" who emphasized charismatic gifts from the Spirit, the Reformers emphasized that God's ordinary way of acting is through the Word read and proclaimed, and the Spirit comes with, not without, the Word.

If, on the other hand, the Spirit comes directly from the Father, this seems to suggest at a symbolic level that the Spirit is "free," not bound by earthly means and ministries; charismatic gifts are not controlled by those who hold office in the church; prophecy, spiritual insight, and the role of women can have a role independent of the male hierarchy. The Spirit "blows where it wills" (John 3:8 RSV), and human authorities cannot trace where it comes from and where it goes. Similarly, if the Spirit moves freely beyond the sphere of the Christian church, new insights might be expected to come from other religions.

The Incarnation

The doctrine of incarnation was likewise a matter of uncertainty when Augustine was baptized in 387. He says in the *Confessions* that he thought of Christ as a man born of a virgin, wiser than all others, but not the Truth in person; then he discovered that this was the heresy of Photinus. His friend Alypius was under the impression that Christ was "God clothed in flesh," not needing a human mind; then he discovered that this was the heresy of Apollinarius.[5]

Augustine affirmed that Christ is both Word and man and that the man consists of mind and soul and body. The question was how to affirm complete humanity and complete divinity without speaking of two persons, two Sons of God. Here as well, Augustine learned from the answer given a few decades earlier by Gregory Nazianzen, who in turn got it from Origen. When the Word becomes flesh, Jesus' mind or spirit is the medium of union: it is joined with the Word with such immediacy of awareness and intensity of love that it becomes like the Word in every respect, like iron heated in fire. This approach was buttressed by a theory picked up from Porphyry, one of the neo-Platonists. To answer the Stoics' question how an immaterial soul could interact with a material body, he used the metaphor of a mixture in which two substances interpenetrate without losing their character. Christian theologians went on to argue that, if material and immaterial things can unite, it is even more obvious that two immaterial things, the divine Word and the human mind, can unite, like sunlight permeating the atmosphere.[6]

Toward the end of his career Augustine emphasized the humanity of Christ more strongly than ever. In defending his doctrine of predestination and prevenient grace, he pointed out that Christ is the chief example of both, united with the Word by the grace of the Holy Spirit from the first moment.[7] But this needed clarification. It is not that Christ was first created and then assumed; he was created by being assumed.[8] Because predestination is "in Christ," Augustine affirmed that believers and Christ are aided by the same grace, namely the Holy Spirit, active in one way in Christ's birth, in another way in their own rebirth. In both cases, furthermore, grace is received by faith. Mary, in responding to Gabriel's announcement by saying "Let it be" (Luke 1:38), conceives Christ by faith, not desire; analogously, Christian rebirth comes through hearing and believing.

Augustine's insistence on two natures in one person was adopted by Leo, pope in the mid-fifth century, who used his language in the so-called tome sent to the Council of Chalcedon (451). This in turn influenced the council's doctrinal declaration, which is shared by the Western and the Eastern Orthodox churches, though not by other Eastern churches. Those that follow Cyril of Alexandria emphasize Christ's unity of person and are accused of confusing the natures; those that follow Nestorius emphasize the difference of natures and are accused of losing his unity of person. In our own day all these churches are engaged in dialogue, trying to understand rather than condemn each other.

While the "person" of Christ is important, the incarnation occurs for the sake of his "work," his function in salvation. Christ is *mediator*, both in his divinity (for all God's actions are "through" the Word) and in his humanity (the "one mediator" is said in 1 Tim 2:5 to be "the man Christ Jesus"). In thinking about this, Augustine was helped, once again, by the Platonists. They thought of a mediator not as something "between" the two extremes, for there ought to be "nothing between" God and the soul (see ch. 2), but as having characteristics of *both* extremes, united immediately. In the case of the incarnation, God is unchangeable and righteous, humanity is changeable and unrighteous, and Christ in his humanity is changeable and righteous.[9]

The purpose of the incarnation, of course, is the salvation of a sinful humanity, which is completed in Christ's death and resurrection. When Augustine reflected on how this happens, he gave several responses.

1. The cross is *revelatory and transformative*. It is the ultimate expression of God's love for sinful humanity, a rebuke to human pride; when confronted with human rebellion and violence it even suffers on the cross. When human beings see the extent of God's love, it touches the depths of their affections and evokes gratitude and love for God. Here we have once again a "moral influence" theory of grace. This line of reflection is found as early as the New Testament (2 Cor 8:9, Phil 2:5-11); it was a major theme in the preaching of Ambrose and Augustine—and of Pelagius; it was emphasized by Abelard in the Middle Ages and by liberal theology in modern times. Its classic expression is in a Spanish sonnet written by an Augustinian and published in Madrid in 1638; it goes this way in Edward Caswall's paraphrase:

> My God, I love Thee, not because
> I hope for Heav'n thereby:
> Nor because they, who love Thee not,
> Must burn eternally.
> . . . .
> Not with the hope of gaining ought;
> Not seeking a reward;
> But, as Thyself hast loved me,
> O ever-loving Lord.[10]

2. The cross is *sacrifice*. There are several kinds of sacrifice in the Bible, but what links them is the attempt to repair one's relationship with God by sacrificing something of value, symbolically sacrificing oneself in total dedication. Augustine thinks of Christ as at once the priest, the offering, and (in his divinity) the recipient of sacrifice.[11]

3. The cross is *ransom*. Here the problem is not God's justice or wrath but the bondage of human beings to death, the law, and the powers of evil. They cannot be freed without a ransom, for the devil has a legiti-

mate claim over sinners. But the devil blundered by abusing this power in the case of Christ; the deceiver is deceived. Those who attach themselves to Christ through baptism and make the sign of the cross, reminding the powers of evil of the one clear instance in which they were discredited, are freed from bondage. Augustine expresses the way ransom works in a memorable way at the end of Book IX of the *Confessions*, speaking of Monica at the eucharistic table:

> She will not claim that she has no debt to pay, lest she be convicted and seized by the cunning accuser. She will reply that her debt has been remitted to her by him to whom no one can repay the price that he, who owed nothing, paid for us.[12]

In liberation theology there is a similar concern with structures of evil that hold people in bondage through both force and deception. When there is undeserved suffering, as in cases like genocide or, on a lesser scale, civil disobedience, the dominating powers are discredited and forfeit any moral authority. The "logic of punishment" reaches its limit and is broken, yielding to an alternative approach based on reconciliation. Yet if we try to make too much of our own righteousness we fall once again under the shadow of judgment. This "logic of justification" is shared by Catholicism and Protestantism, and it has its roots in late Jewish reflections about undeserved suffering that is vindicated by God (Wis 2:12-20, 5:1-8, which probably influenced Phil 2:5-11). René Girard even claims that there is a critique of "scapegoating violence" throughout the Bible, in both the Old Testament and the New.[13]

Questions for Reflection

1. How helpful is Augustine's comparison of the Trinity with the human mind?

2. What difference does it make whether the Spirit comes "from the Father" or "from the Father and the Son"? Where do you come down on this question?

3. Summarize and reflect on the many ways in which, for Augustine, both the "person" and the "work" of Christ manifest divine love.

CHAPTER EIGHT

CITIZENS AND SOJOURNERS: LIVING IN TWO CITIES

The Goths under Alaric began wandering through the western provinces in 401 and entered Italy in 408; many who could afford it fled to Sicily and to Africa, even before Rome was sacked in 410. This, Augustine tells us, was the immediate occasion for writing *The City of God*, answering pagan charges that the disaster was the result of Rome's forsaking its traditional rituals. The full title is *On the City of God against the Pagans*.

But Augustine goes far beyond the scope of an "occasional" work. In the first ten books he refutes the epic of Rome, using the *Aeneid*, the Roman historians, and the Greek philosophers to criticize the Romans and their religion. Then he writes twelve more books, an alternative epic of the human race as it is presented in the Bible and Christian doctrine.[1]

He had to rethink the relationship of Christianity to the political world. For a decade and more he had celebrated "Christian times," the result of Theodosius's suppression of paganism and heresy in the 390s. His language was triumphalist: there is only one way of salvation, and it spread throughout the world even before emperors became Christian; now emperors are obeying the divine command to destroy idols, fulfilling the prophecy that God's name will be praised from the rising to the setting of the sun.

There are modern parallels. The worldwide missionary activity of the nineteenth and twentieth centuries seemed to be a similar confirmation of God's promises (it was linked, of course, with Western imperialism, just as Christianity's early expansion was aided by the Roman Empire). Or consider the more cautious optimism of the Christian West after the Second World War. Fascism had been defeated and discredited; churches in the United States rediscovered their European roots, with special admiration for figures like Dietrich Bonhoeffer and Karl Barth; the World Council of Churches brought together the Orthodox churches, the mainline Protestant churches, and the "younger churches" in the non-Western world that had been founded by Western missionaries and were now becoming self-governing. Then fissures began to appear. Colonial empires gave way to independent governments; the World Council of Churches was rivaled by the "Lausanne group" of missionary organizations; and when hopes for economic development were disappointed they often gave rise to liberation movements and liberation theology.

Today the spirit of triumphalism is more likely to be found among evangelicals, who point out that the fastest-growing churches are in Africa and parts of Asia. When there are disputes in the churches of Europe and the United States over the ordination of gay and lesbian persons, conservative evangelicals welcome the opposition that comes from churches in the Third World—an area, ironically, with which liberals so often like to profess their solidarity—and predict with glee that the liberalism of the churches in Europe and the United States will be overwhelmed by the growing number of Christians in other parts of the world and by their immigration into Europe and the United States.[2]

Examples like these may help us sympathize with Augustine and others in the age of Theodosius, who, unrealistically as it turned out, found fulfillment of prophecy and assurance about the future in what was happening around them.

In 410 "Christian times" suddenly turned sour; the expression was now used by pagan critics in listing the disasters that happened on the Christians' watch. Augustine developed a new political theology, though gradually and with many hesitations—one that did not tie the destiny of Catholic Christianity so closely to the fortunes of the Roman Empire. It was an approach that turned out to be uncannily relevant in the coming centuries, first under the new Germanic rulers, then during the disputes in the Middle Ages over the freedom of the church from secular rulers. The differentiation of church and state that developed in the West stands in contrast with their close linkage in Byzantium and the Eastern Church. The contrast was intensified by a number of doctrinal disputes from the 500s to the 800s; several times the popes in Rome broke communion with Constantinople over doctrinal issues, and their spirit of independence was soon transferred to their dealings with European rulers.

When the ancients engaged in political theory, starting in Athens, they thought in terms of cities, not kingdoms; and that was Augustine's paradigm too. For him the first and best city of God already exists in the heavens; it consists, quite simply, of the angels. They are God's first creation. They themselves are "heaven," the "city" or "house" of God, in whom God dwells through knowledge and love.[3] The original city, then, is made not of bricks and mortar but of lucid minds and fervent wills.

The human race was created to be in training for the celestial city, differing from the angels in being subject to generation and growth, which also means that after they sin they, unlike the rebel angels, have the possibility of repentance. During this training, humanity was to have a "social" life; descent from a single person would be an inducement to unity and concord through family affection. But things did not turn out that way. It was Cain, the fratricide, who founded the first city (Gen 4:17). All of us are born in the lineage of Cain, citizens of the earthly city. But we can also be reborn, as Abel was, becoming citizens of the heavenly city, which is symbolized on earth by Jerusalem.

In the midst of the earthly city, then, there are those who are not fully at home in it but look for another city. The earthly city is ambivalent, usable by people with both sets of motivations. (Augustine likes to say that earthly things, earthly activities and achievements, are "referred" to different ends, basically either God or self.) Even those who have been reborn as citizens of the heavenly city remain earthbound. With their change of loyalties they have become strangers and sojourners in the earthly city, which is figuratively Babylon, not Jerusalem.

In the ancient world, sojourners, while they were foreign-born, were not simply aliens, for they had certain rights, differing from city to city. Augustine's favorite text for describing Christians as sojourners is Paul's statement (2 Cor 5:6-7), "As long as we are in the body we sojourn away from the Lord, for we walk by faith, not by sight." It is a sojourning *away from* God, Christ, the heavenly city, the peace of God. The sojourn is *within the earthly city*, in territory quite different from what is hoped for. Christians in our own day have revived this image of strangers and sojourners as a description of radical discipleship within the earthly city.

The term *city* refers in the first ten books of *The City of God* to earthly cities, especially Babylon and Rome, the greatest empires; in the last twelve books it comes to be used metaphorically. The two loves and the two societies based on them *transcend* all observable states and organizations. Augustine emphasizes that each city is made up of both angels and human beings; thus there are *two cities, not four*. It is precisely because the human spirit transcends earthly things, is laden with meanings that reach far beyond physical events and relationships, that spiritual values cannot be adequately expressed in political life. Early in his career Augustine had opposed *theoretical* Manichaeism; now he opposes *practical* Manichaeism as well.

This statement must immediately be clarified. While Augustine did not think good and evil could be identified in a tangible way, he did think in terms of *spiritual* warfare between forces of good and evil, truth and deception; between the angels who dwell in the highest heaven and the "spiritual hosts of wickedness in high places" (Eph 6:12), who are *not* in the highest heaven but inhabit the stormy realm of the atmosphere (Eph 2:2) and are under the direction of Satan, the deceiver. Both angels and demons are constantly calling to the human self and to human society. The warfare is not Manichaean, with good and evil clearly identifiable; it is spiritual in character, communicated through signs. And that is a large part of the problem. The signs in Scripture reveal God's promises; but even these can be misinterpreted. And the signs used in the religions of the Gentiles at best refer to the physical elements, at worst become the vehicle for deception by the demons, the false mediators.[4] Spiritual conflict runs through the middle of every community and every person. The overtones are as multivalent as our modern notion of *ideology*: political doctrines claim to champion what is true, just, and good, but they are more likely to be vehicles of deception and "false consciousness."

Despite the spiritual distance between the two cities, which are figuratively Jerusalem and Babylon, Augustine found guidance in Jeremiah's advice to the exiles in Babylon (Jer 29:7): seek the peace or welfare—*shalom*—of the city where you are, for in its peace you will find your peace. Its peace, to be sure, is the peace of Babylon, the earthly city. And yet it is to be accepted gratefully, because the peace of the earthly city can be shared by the citizens of both cities.

Not too much is to be expected of the earthly city. It is not motivated by love for God and neighbor; it permits all sorts of acts as long as they involve consenting adults.[5] It has its own kind of justice, one that punishes sinners not when they love earthly things but when they take these things away from others.[6] There need not be agreement about basic values. (On this point Augustine would disagree with modern-day "communitarians.") The earthly city concerns itself with externals. Yet the peace of Babylon, for precisely this reason, contributes to the living out of the Christian life. If we need chapter and verse, Augustine finds it in Jesus' statement to the disciples, "Peace I leave with you; my peace I give to you" (John 14:27 RSV). The first is not Christ's peace but the world's peace; yet Christ also conferred this peace upon them, for it, too, is worth having.[7]

Augustine's influence on church-state relations in the West has been varied. He supported the actions of the Christian emperors. If the apostles did not seek the support of rulers to defend the church against its enemies, it was only because in their day the nations still raged and rulers rose up against God and God's anointed (Ps 2:1-2). In his own day the prophecy was at last fulfilled that rulers would serve God (Ps 2:10-11). There were precedents in Hezekiah and Josiah, who destroyed idols and enforced God's law.[8]

Augustine could say with equanimity, "Always the evil have perse-cuted the good and the good have persecuted the evil"—the former unjustly, violently, and selfishly, the latter justly, temperately, and for their good.[9] He was impatient with those who thought that sinful wills ought to be given freedom of choice[10]; during both the Donatist and the Pelagian controversies he appreciated the coercive hand of government. In this respect he anticipates the attitude of those in the nineteenth cen-tury who held that "error does not have the same rights as truth," or those in our own time who complain that civil liberties simply "abandon peo-ple to their own desires."

His differentiation between the two cities gave theological backing, however, to other approaches to politics. The intensity of the contrast between the city of God and the earthly city, with the former having far greater dignity, led in the Middle Ages to what has been called "political Augustinianism," the assertion of the church's superiority over rulers and its right to discipline or depose them. The same contrast also has its obverse side, a despairing or cynical acceptance of the earthly city, the "political realism" associated most closely with Reinhold Niebuhr. From this per-spective, individuals and governments are more likely to respond to self-interest than to appeals to justice, and they are to be dealt with accordingly.

While anticipations of each of these positions can be found in Augustine, his most explicit development of a political theory is in Book XIX of *The City of God*, probably written in 425. It forms the beginning of the last part of the work, dealing with the "ends" (values, goals, destinies) of the two cities. Here he says nothing about the use of the power of the state to aid the cause of true religion. He may still wel-come it (he had recently benefited from the empire's condemnation of Pelagianism); it may still belong to the actual *functions* of the state; but it is clearly incidental to its *purposes*. With many delays and detours, mutterings and internal conflicts, he develops a position that amounts to a defense of what we call the "secular state."[11] He is talking about the earthly city, after all, the city of the earthborn, whose life is shared by the twice-born.

The West, aided partly by Augustine as he thought about the earthly city but principally by the heritage of Roman law, has generally seen the purpose of the state as a "secular" one. This position is buttressed by authorities like Thomas Aquinas on the Catholic side and Martin Luther on the Protestant, against others who advocated a more direct Christian regulation of the state. The Thirty Years' War finally exhausted the patience of Europe with wars of religion and brought fresh appreciation for the secular state.

The West has learned to differentiate between *church and state* as institutions, even while refusing to separate *religion and politics*, since we know that religious concerns are relevant to the whole of life. More crucially, we have learned the value of the *secular state* that has no official ties with any religious institutions but guarantees *religious freedom*, including the right to change religions or have no religion.

Of course this does not keep religious zealots from trying to influence political life directly; then we find ourselves in the midst of what James Davison Hunter calls "culture wars." Hunter suggests that culture wars have an intrinsic tendency toward Manichaean thinking: they are based in competing moral visions, with the result that those who disagree are placed beyond the bounds of legitimacy,[12] and there is an urge to "force political solutions" rather than trust continued dialogue.[13]

In a First-Amendment society, it is easy for religious people to believe that religion is the only thing that "gets no respect." Any excesses on the part of the Religious Right are then regarded as an understandable reaction to a relentlessly "secular" government. To prove their point they engage in provocative acts such as putting the Ten Commandments on stone in public places or passing out tracts in public schools, then cry persecution when objections are raised. Such actions are defended, furthermore, with the argument that religion is an "absolute commitment," as though this makes it exempt from the rules of political behavior and even confers the privilege of defining those rules. The problem, of course, is that many competing religious groups can claim the right to carry their "absolute commitments" into the public sphere; this encourages intolerance and eventually open religious warfare. Thus the West has chosen to keep absolute claims out of the public square and develop a viable "secular state," while not denying that religious commitments are always relevant to issues of human good.[14]

Augustine had celebrated the coercive measures of Christian emperors. He continued to appreciate the role played by the court in turning the tide against the Pelagians in 418. But his last word on the subject, in Book XIX of *The City of God*, was an acknowledgment that citizens of the heavenly city have much to share with citizens of the earthly city.

He had experienced the way each of these "spiritual cities" expressed its convictions in the public square, first with pagans persecuting Christians, then with Christians persecuting pagans. The risks are all the greater because these "spiritual cities" have transcendent value commitments, for they include not only human beings but angels and demons. That kind of spiritual warfare is an invitation to trouble when it seeks political expression. Now he saw that the two cities might more profitably seek better ways of living together in the public square.

Questions for Reflection

1. Augustine had to deal with several dramatic shifts in the political situation of Christianity during his career as a churchman. How, and why, did his views change? Did his opinions improve?

2. Augustine refused to identify the "city of God" and the "earthly city" with tangible communities; instead he saw them as "spiritual" in character, communicated through signs and responded to in the center of the self. How might this help us in thinking about politics, and about the Christian life, today?

3. What relation of church and state makes best sense today in (a) the United States, (b) the European countries, (c) countries settled by Europeans, and (d) countries that are predominantly non-Christian and non-Western?

CHAPTER NINE

THE SUNSET YEARS: CREATING A HERITAGE

In the fall of 418, just after the triumph of seeing Pelagianism condemned by the empire and the pope, Augustine took his longest journey. He and Alypius and Possidius went as papal legates to Caesarea Mauretania in the far west (modern Cherchell in Algeria), closer to Spain than to Carthage. Perhaps the pope was letting Augustine make amends for a doctrinal victory in which the pope had been the loser. Perhaps the Africans accepted the task because it would be executed by themselves, not by legates from Rome. Perhaps Augustine was letting Rome take primary responsibility for dealing with difficult matters, including the continued intransigence of the Donatist bishop Emeritus.[1] What is clear is that the Africans were not subservient toward Rome. In 419 Alypius, the lawyer turned bishop, trumped a papal legate by proving that they had a better version of the canons of Nicaea than Rome's.

The long journey to the west and back, in the wagons of the imperial post, probably gave Augustine an opportunity for reading and writing, discussions with his two colleagues, and comprehensive reflection. When he came home, at the age of 64, his literary activity took a new form; he began completing the corpus of his writings, preparing his testament to future generations.

It was after 418 that he finished his expository sermons on the Psalms and the Gospel according to John, even dictating some of them. He completed his major work, *On the Trinity*. He reworked some sermons on practical themes (patience, continence, lying, care for the dead, faith in the unseen), circulating them as popular tracts. This was also when he wrote the historical books of *The City of God* (XV–XVIII), doing extensive research on the narratives in the Old Testament. The concluding section on the destiny of the two cities (XIX–XXII) would be written in 425–427. In his final years he compiled the *Speculum*, gathering together all the ethical commands and counsels in scripture.

By 422 he had written his *Enchiridion* or "handbook," the closest he ever came to a comprehensive presentation of his views, quite different from medieval and modern "systematic theologies." It was built around the creed, the Lord's Prayer, and the Ten Commandments, basic texts for Christian instruction; but there were many detours to discuss issues that were being debated at the time, such as sin and evil, predestination and grace, and free choice. The creed's mention of God's omnipotence, for example, led to a lengthy discussion of redemption and God's permission of evil.

In this work we see Augustine paying much attention to pastoral issues and themes in popular piety. His discussion of "forgiveness of sins" touches on baptism, the church's penitential discipline, the meaning of the "unforgivable sin" against the Holy Spirit (Matt 12:32), the necessity of almsgiving for salvation, purification of sinners after death through fire (1 Cor 3:10-15), care for the dead and prayers for the dead.

This was the time, too, when he asked Paulinus, a deacon from Milan, to write a life of Ambrose, on the model of the earlier lives written by Athanasius on Antony, Jerome on Paul of Thebes (the legendary "first hermit"), and Severus on Martin of Tours. Popular piety was a force worth harnessing.

On saints' days the custom was to read the narrative of martyrdom in the church along with passages of scripture, and the sermon connected all these things with the life of the congregation. Augustine now began to devote much effort to publicizing the miracles wrought in his own time by the relics of Saint Stephen. These had been discovered in Palestine during the Eastern synod of Diospolis, where several Westerners, including Orosius of Braga, accused Pelagius of heresy, but to their dismay he was acquitted. There was considerable Western involvement in the discovery of the relics, and it has long been suspected that a fellow presbyter, Avitus of Braga, wrote the narrative and a supposed Greek original was only a "cover story." According to the narrative, both Stephen and Nicodemus had been buried by the converted rabbi Gamaliel, and their bodies were discovered about twenty miles from Jerusalem through a dream given to a certain Lucianus.

Relics were not yet divided up, at least in the West (Roman culture had a strong taboo against disturbing corpses, and it was enforced by law). It was enough to have a cloth that had been let down into the grave or a drop of oil or a flower from the altar. Holiness was conferred through contagion, yes, but more by symbolic reference. In the case of Stephen, however, all that had been found were a few bones and some dust, and it is possible that some of the actual remains were brought to the West in 416 and were parceled out to those who requested them. Two of Augustine's fellow bishops seized the opportunity. The relics not only produced miracles but became an important source of validation when Catholic bishops dealt with former Donatists.

Hippo did not secure relics of Saint Stephen until 424, and this was at the initiative of Eraclius, a wealthy presbyter who would succeed Augustine as bishop. Now Augustine, with the thoroughness of an intellectual, documented the miracles wrought through the saint and compiled them in a long chapter in the last book of *The City of God*. During one of his sermons he even brought to the front, as living documentation, a man who had been healed.

During his last decade, in the midst of promoting popular piety, Augustine also devoted plenty of time to intellectual tasks. He continued his long literary battle with Julian of Eclanum, the persistent advocate of Pelagianism. There were also more neutral but still puzzled inquiries about his emphasis on grace and predestination, to which he responded in two double works. *On Grace and Free Choice* and *On Rebuke and Grace* replied to questions from a monastery near Hadrumetum, on the coast south of Carthage; *On the Predestination of Saints* and *On the Gift of Perseverance* answered questions from a monastery near Marseilles, where John Cassian was abbot. John Burnaby famously criticized these works as an expression of "love grown cold."[2] His judgment is not widely shared. These works contain some of Augustine's deepest and gentlest reflections. He makes the famous contrast between the grace given to Adam and Eve, which they could freely continue to receive, and the grace offered to sinners, which makes possible their free response. He advises preachers to hold out hope for grace and not mention the possibility of the hearers' being rejected.[3] In response to people who are anxious about what God intends for them, he asks whether they know what their own changeable wills have in store for them.[4] Knowing the hazards of temporality, he prefers God's faithfulness to our own.

In the last four books of *The City of God*, written during the years 425–427, he reached theoretical closure, dealing with "the last things," including the contrasting "ends" of the two cities. When he looked at the eschatology of the Apocalypse, with its anticipation of an earthly reign of Christ (Rev 20), triumphalism was gone. He reinterpreted it in a Pauline direction: the only millennium there will ever be is the present time, during which believers, to be sure, reign with Christ, but only in the midst of struggle with themselves and their spiritual enemies, awaiting the release of Satan for a final round of persecution that will demonstrate how mighty an adversary they, through Christ, have conquered.[5] His optimism is like that of Churchill during the Battle of Britain, or of Kierkegaard's Knight of Faith, or of Luther's "Here I stand" in front of Charles V and the Reichstag, at a time when all parties were aware of the threat from the Turks on the plains of Hungary.

Perhaps Augustine turned toward popular piety, relics, and miracles as a substitute for government coercion, shifting sanctions for good behavior and hopes for the future from the state to the church. Something like this is suggested by his discussion, in the paradoxical manner of a Paul or a Tertullian, of the "incredibility" of the Christian faith, specifically the resurrection of Christ. If this is incredible, he says, then let us make the most of it. It is also incredible that the whole world should have believed such an incredible thing; and it is incredible, furthermore, that the world should have been persuaded by a few simple men with no education. Thus we have not one but *three* incredible things. If we leave aside the resurrection of Christ and the miracles of the apostles (for these are open to historical doubt[6]), there is still the "one great miracle" that in enlightened times the whole world, without seeing miracles and in the midst of persecution and martyrdom, has believed a faith that seemed incredible. (In more recent times apologists have called this the "moral miracle" of Christianity's spread.) In fact, then, this faith is not incredible, for it has been believed throughout the world; if it seemed incredible at first, that was only because it was new and unaccustomed, not because it was contrary to reason.[7] But then Augustine went on, only a few chapters later, to discuss the miracles wrought through Saint Stephen. Was he throwing his point away? It is more likely that, having said that the world has believed *without* manifest miracles, he wanted to show that there are even more reasons to believe *with* these miracles in his own time.

During his last decade Augustine took pains to preserve his writings and send copies to other places. He also compiled a list of them, which is probably the basis of the *Indiculus* or *Indiculum* that Possidius appended to the biography he wrote after Augustine's death. Most of the writings are classified under controversies—with the pagans, the Manichees, the Donatists, the Pelagians, the Arians—and then there are those written "for the use of all inquirers," something always worth doing, but a luxury in the midst of so many pressing disputes. Augustine also surveyed and evaluated his literary output in a work entitled *Reconsiderations*. This has been valuable to historians in telling us the sequence of his writings. In a manuscript culture like that of the Middle Ages, it was a useful catalog to his writings. And as O'Donnell points out, it became Augustine's self-presentation to coming centuries, akin to the *Confessions*.[8] For theorists interested in the workings of "textuality," it is the first major example of a text reevaluating other texts by the same author and exhibiting his second thoughts.

Augustine died on August 28, 430, with the Vandals at the gates of Hippo. After besieging it for a time, they went on. A few years later their leader Gaiseric made it his capital; thus it could not have been heavily damaged. Possidius was expelled from Africa in 437, and at that time or soon afterward Augustine's library was transported to Rome. It clearly influenced Pope Leo I (440–461), and as Augustine's works spread he became the chief influence on doctrine, ethics, and monastic life in the West. It is not inappropriate, then, that representations of Augustine, starting with the fresco painted in the late sixth century in the Lateran, depicted him as a writer, holding a codex or a scroll or both. That, rather than the beleaguered church in Vandal-dominated North Africa, was his legacy.

Let us remind ourselves of the changes that occurred during Augustine's lifetime. He had been born in 354, an era of religious pluralism. It was only during the 380s, the decade of his conversion, that old disputes about the Trinity and about Christ reached anything like a lasting resolution, doctrinally and politically. The major turning point in the relation between church and state came not with Constantine in 312 and 324, but with Theodosius in the 390s, the decade during which Augustine became a bishop. Classical culture, the Roman Empire, and Christianity drew closer together, especially because the empire was threatened by the Goths, Christians but of the Arian variety, which was considered heretical. The Catholic Church had every reason to appreciate both Greek culture and the Roman Empire, from which paganism had now been banished.

Optimism faded when the Goths invaded the West in 401 and sacked Rome in 410. The legions were withdrawn from Britain in 407, leaving Britain and Ireland to Celtic Christianity for the next two centuries. Now Africa, already the chief source of grain for Rome, became the most secure base of military power in the West. This may have helped Augustine and several African councils take a firm and independent position at the height of the Pelagian controversy, and it may be one reason the court in Ravenna sided with Augustine against the Pelagians in 418. (Galla Placidia, whose mausoleum in Ravenna has become famous, was a daughter of Theodosius, forced to marry a Gothic leader. Released after his death in 415, she married the military commander Constantius; both of them were firm supporters of Augustine.) Africa's advantage ended in 429 when the Vandals, another Germanic group, crossed from Spain into Africa, ending Roman rule there. Augustine was a transitional figure in many ways, sharing personally in the change from one epoch to another.

Questions for Reflection

1. Karl Jaspers pointed out that Augustine, Kierkegaard, and Nietzsche all placed great importance on writing as an expression of themselves, were not afraid of change or inconsistency, and engaged in retrospective

examination of their own writings. What does this suggest about the relation of life and thought, at least in some thinkers?

2. Augustine took a much-sobered view of political life and the earthly future during his last decade. At the same time he placed much greater emphasis on popular piety. What are the benefits and the dangers of an attitude like this?

CHAPTER TEN

FOOTNOTES, QUERIES, AND OBITUARIES TO AUGUSTINE

A lfred North Whitehead once said that Western philosophy is a series of footnotes to Plato. However that may be, it is certainly true that Western doctrine is a series of footnotes, commentaries, and questions to Augustine. Many have found him worthy of examination. Dissertations were written on him by Hannah Arendt (1929) and by Albert Camus (1936), a fellow North African, although neither can be called a disciple. There have also been many who want to bury him, attending to him largely to see where he went wrong.

Influence

Augustine's writings gave distinctive shape to a number of doctrines in the West: Trinity and incarnation, church and sacraments, original sin, grace and free will. His views were not accepted uncritically. Especially when it came to original sin, predestination, and prevenient grace, his views were softened within a hundred years after his death, both in Rome and in the area that would soon become France.

Augustine's rule for the monastery in Hippo, combining contemplation with the "active life" of the clergy, spread throughout southern Europe and became the basis for the office of "canons," priests in cathedrals or collegiate churches who lived together and engaged in ministry to the faithful. They claimed to combine the best of both monks and priests, teaching by both example and word. The Augustinian rule was adopted by the Dominicans and other orders. It was also used by many communities of women, starting with the Beguines in the cities of the Rhineland and continuing in the women's communities that were promoted in the seventeenth century by Francis de Sales and came to full expression in the nineteenth century, engaging in many kinds of service to the world through orphanages, schools, and hospitals.

When Peter Lombard compiled his *Sentences*, lining up authoritative statements from the "fathers and doctors" of the church on various issues of theology, about 90 percent of the passages were from Augustine. The *Sentences* became the standard textbook of theology in medieval universities, shaping the topics chosen for disputations and supplying at least the starting arguments. The Augustinian perspective was never adopted uncritically. With the study of Aristotle, Augustine's Platonism was questioned, most notably by Thomas Aquinas. And yet it was Aquinas who, after discovering some of Augustine's last writings that had not been used by Lombard, gave new emphasis to predestination and grace.

During the Renaissance, Augustine was the principal model of Christian use of classical culture. Petrarch, the first symbol of the new study of the humanities, always carried a pocket-sized copy of the *Confessions*. Renaissance figures like Ficino and Pico, Vives and Colet and Erasmus used Augustine's authority to reassert Plato against Aristotle, mystical inwardness against the authority of the church, and the essay style against scholasticism with its close-packed argumentation. These same thinkers were not sympathetic, however, with other aspects of Augustine, especially his views on original sin, the bondage of the will, the need for grace, and predestination; here Erasmus openly preferred Origen to Augustine.

The founder of modern philosophy, Descartes, made experience his starting point. In his case it meant assuming nothing about external reality and turning inward; his argument "I think, therefore I am" is based on Augustine's "I doubt, therefore I am." The eighteenth-century interest in the moral affections and benevolent love (seen especially in Shaftesbury, Hutcheson, and Edwards) is in a trajectory started by Augustine. In all these respects Adolf von Harnack was right when he said that Augustine was "the first modern man."

During the Reformation era, Catholics emphasized Augustine's doctrine of the church and his interest in various aspects of popular piety, including his incipient doctrine of purgatory; Protestants emphasized what he said about bondage to sin and the need for grace.

In both the Catholic and the Protestant traditions there were disputes about free will and grace that were basically attempts to reclaim Augustine. The Jansenists and many of the Calvinists emphasized efficacious grace; the Jesuits and the Edwardsians sought formulations that would show how grace does not overcome free choice but works with it. Steadily the spirit of the Enlightenment moved beyond both tendencies and emphasized the potentialities of the human spirit itself. But this, too, was an Augustinian emphasis, the framework for his more detailed reflections on will and grace.

Critiques

Precisely because he is a major teacher of the West, Augustine has been subjected to intense scrutiny and often to outspoken criticism.

Feminists justly complain that, even though his view of women was more positive than that of many others in his age, he gave authority to the assumption that women are naturally inferior and a source of temptation.

Heidegger and Derrida and other post-structuralists criticize him for his "metaphysics of presence," his attempt to find in God a unity and stability that are not to be found either in oneself or in the sensory world or in human culture. It is not that Augustine was unaware of change. Like others in the tradition of Plato, he saw it everywhere in the world and in human experience; indeed, he emphasized the fluidity and instability of all that is created, and the kaleidoscopic character of sense experience, using them to argue for the reality of a higher realm unthreatened by change. Derrida is, in effect, a Platonist who only has the *chora*, the "receptacle" of formless matter and shifting words, without the ideas or the Demiurge to give stability. (A middle ground, likewise in the Platonist tradition, is process theology, which begins with the fact of constant change but credits God, also a participant in the cosmic process, with continuity and order in the world.)

William Connolly, in the tradition of Nietzsche and Foucault, focuses on the more affective aspects. He finds in Augustine's guilt over original sin and in his magnifying of grace a hatred of—even a "revenge against"—the human condition, a denial of vulnerability and death and oblivion. Confession and repentance only intensify the double bind, enabling Augustine to acknowledge guilt and inability, give glory not to himself but to God, and then assume the role of humble servant to this God of power, justice, and mercy, ready to enforce all that this God reveals and blame everyone from Adam to contemporaneous pagans, heretics, and schismatics for the disorder that plagues human society and even the church. More scholarly critiques along much the same lines have been mounted by Elaine Pagels and Kurt Flasch. If we listen to them, Augustine paved the way toward Dostoyevsky's Grand Inquisitor, who thinks that freedom produces so much anxiety and uncertainty that human beings will prefer miracle over responsibility, mystery over understanding, and authority over conscience.

Augustine's psychological processes can indeed be diagnosed, in the manner of Feuerbach and Nietzsche, as projecting all one's capabilities onto God, then receiving them back in the form of revelation and grace. He did experience the whole range of conflicts that Connolly evokes. He declared intellectual independence at the age of nineteen, found increasingly exalted goals to strive for, and set high standards for himself; but then the experience of his own inability led him to renounce the claims of both the intellect ("unless you believe you will not understand") and the will (true freedom is conferred only by grace). All of this may indeed arouse our suspicion.

Let us also note, however, the positive contributions Augustine made to Western thought and religion. He recovered a more relational and more affective view of the self, criticizing self-assertiveness because it involves loss of community with God, with other intelligent beings, and with the whole of creation. His posture was one of openness to the world, honesty about his own errors, and gratitude for the many positive things that come to us from outside ourselves. He often quoted Paul's statement that we have only what we have received (1 Cor 4:7). To receive them is to make them ours. But if we claim them as our own or hoard them, we will lose them. Gift must be answered with self-giving.

Augustine's Inner Conflicts

Augustine was quite willing to acknowledge that he had changed his views on a variety of questions; both his *Confessions* and his *Reconsiderations* are full of specifics. Historians have also tried to trace his inner conflicts, for there were issues over which he quarreled with himself.

1. The *most personal* had to do with Manichaeism. He had been attracted to its fatalistic view that evil in the world and in oneself is the result of an evil nature mixed with the good. Rejecting its attempt to make good and evil tangible substances, he developed the "privation" theory of evil; against its fatalism about sin, he defended the freedom of the will. Did he later revert to Manichaeism with his emphasis on original sin and bondage of the will, and especially with his conviction that the "concupiscence of the flesh" is always sinful, though venially so for married couples?

He could show that his statements were based on Paul and meant something quite different from Manichaeism. If sin is unavoidable, he argued, it is still the result of past willing and is never without willing; the present condition of human nature may not be optimal, but it can be transformed by grace. Running close under the guns of both sides of the dispute, he showed how "the Catholic faith" avoids the opposing errors of the Manichaeans and the Pelagians.[1] Schleiermacher would later do the same thing, calling these the two "natural heresies" of the Christian approach to human life.[2]

But questions persist. Did Manichaeism continue to influence his perception of the issues and his mode of approach to them? Were there unconscious tendencies that led him first to Manichaeism and later to bondage of the will? And yet, even if this should be true, it may also be that these unconscious tendencies gave him a deeper awareness of issues that others wanted to avoid, for the true measure of moral integrity and intellectual honesty is a readiness to pursue such problems, verbalize them, and explore their complexities.

2. The *most dramatic* conflict concerns free will and predestination. In his anti-Manichaean writings Augustine defended free choice, and these passages were later quoted against him by Pelagius and Julian. Then he was persuaded by Paul to affirm predestination. And yet, after making this point in 397, he was silent about it for fourteen years, until the issues were raised afresh by the Pelagian controversy.

It could be that his early defense of free choice was an overemphasis, motivated by eagerness to refute the Manichaeans. And it could be that in adopting the predestinarian position he swung to the other extreme, yielding to the authority of Paul without knowing what to do with him.[3] In any case, the Pelagian controversy forced him to clarify his position and bring his various affirmations into a complex harmony.

But the Pelagian controversy also led him to a fateful change in his understanding of human life. Earlier he had been willing to entertain the possibility that its vulnerabilities result not from sin but from the way God created human beings, probably as an inducement to growth. The allies of Pelagius continued to take this position; Julian of Eclanum saw not only mortality but sexual desire as "natural," to be dealt with in reasonable and responsible ways. Augustine at first entertained the developmental perspective, affirming the down-to-earth creation of Adam and Eve and thinking of God's call to the angels as an offer of something better than their created condition. Later he turned against it, on the grounds that it is inappropriate for created beings to make themselves better than God made them, even if they are responding to grace. The result was that all human vulnerabilities came to be viewed as consequences of a primal fall. Such a perspective was not unusual in the ancient world, where life in a vast and complex empire could be full of frustrations and disappointments, and where Platonists, Gnostics, and Manichaeans seemed to offer plausible explanations for the deep shadows that haunt human life.

The broader question to which these various answers were given is this: what is the relation of God's creative activity to the vulnerabilities of human life? For Gnostics, Manichaeans, and Origenists, in quite different ways, the creation of the world *follows* a fall in the spiritual realm. For the later Augustine, creation *precedes* a fall into vulnerability. For the earlier Augustine (at least in some moods), the Pelagians, and most moderns, creation and human vulnerability occur *in parallel*, and it may be difficult to sort them out.

3. What is perhaps Augustine's *most consequential* inner conflict has to do with the relation of church and state. When he began his career as a presbyter and then a bishop, he had the philosopher's confidence that truth will be persuasive and the Christian's conviction that faith should not be coerced. But imperial measures against paganism, issued in 399, seemed to be an unprecedented fulfillment of prophecy. Soon afterward he saw the need for legal measures to restrain the violence of the Donatists and their followers; in a few more years he was persuaded that coercive measures brought them to their right mind. The Pelagian controversy only deepened his conviction that the sinful will should not be left to its own disordered desires. And imperial intervention against the Pelagians rescued Augustine and his party from probable defeat. In these various ways the actions of the empire seemed not only to fulfill prophecy but to advance the reign of Christ.

The sack of Rome in 410 began to dampen his enthusiasm. Still he continued to defend the measures taken by the empire. It was only late in his life, probably in 425, as he reflected on the aims of the earthly city and the city of God in Book XIX of *The City of God*, that he came to a full appreciation of the earthly city as a space shared by members of both spiritual cities. While he never explicitly rejected government intervention in religious matters, he ceased expressing great hopes for it. The result of these mutations in his thinking is that Augustine became the church father of political philosophies ranging from the Christian state in its various forms to political realism with its calculations of self-interest to the secular state with its potentialities for justice and peace through external, worldly cooperation.

Augustine's understanding of the cosmos is alien to ours. But we share with him a respect for mathematical order, for natural growth, and for the complex relations among all finite things. And we have been constructively influenced by him, especially through his attention to the dynamics of our inner life, which can range all the way from philosophical questions about certitude to concern with the affections and their transformation by grace.

We began with a reminder about the nature of all interpretation. It must start with careful examination of the past and its written expressions. It must continue with an awareness of the way these same issues are important to us. And we must eventually deal with these issues in our own day and give our own answers.

That would be very much in the spirit of Augustine, who was engaged in constant inquiry and reassessment, often laying out a number of alternatives and inviting the reader to think the issues through. He praised Porphyry, a neo-Platonist philosopher, for criticizing Plato on a central point. Here is a Platonist emending Plato, he said, preferring truth to the opinions of Plato, and this is very much in the spirit of Plato.[4] In the midst of his highest-soaring reflections on the Trinity, he warned that even those who find must continue seeking; repeatedly he told his readers, and not simply as a diplomatic nicety, that he would welcome their corrections. This spirit of inquiry is typical of Augustine. It is something that we learn from almost all of his works. And perhaps our chief debt to him is that he urges us not to rest even with his own statements but to continue asking and seeking.

Questions for Reflection

1. Augustine thought of himself as an intellectual, as a member of the worldwide church, and as a sinner in need of grace. How do these fit together? How well can they be separated from each other, as often happened in more recent centuries?

2. Do you find Augustine more valuable because of the *answers* he gave to doctrinal questions or because of the *way he approached them*?

3. On balance, was Augustine's influence on the West a good one or not?

DEFINITIONS

Aeneid: The epic poem by Virgil that tells of the founding of Rome and celebrates its destiny, written ca. 29–19 B.C.E.

Ambrose: Bishop of Milan (374–397) after being governor. He influenced the emperor Theodosius on several occasions and was important in Augustine's conversion.

Arians: A fourth-century movement that regarded the Son as "less than the Father." It was opposed by the Nicene party.

Caelestius: A teacher in Rome, influenced by Rufinus the Syrian; he was the actual focus of most of the condemnations during the Pelagian controversy.

Cappadocians: The three leading theologians of the Greek-speaking church in the late fourth century, all from central Asia Minor: Basil of Caesarea, his brother Gregory of Nyssa, and their friend Gregory Nazianzen.

Cicero (106–43 B.C.E.): Roman orator, statesman, and philosopher; the chief transmitter of Greek philosophy to Latin speakers.

Donatists: A fourth-century group in North Africa that claimed greater purity than the Catholic Church, not only in North Africa but throughout the world.

Goths: A Germanic people that migrated from the Baltic to the steppes of Ukraine, settled south of the Danube, and were often employed as mercenaries in the Roman army; after 401 they invaded Italy, Gaul, and Spain.

Hortensius: A dialogue by Cicero that invites the reader to the philosophic quest for wisdom and happiness; written ca. 45 B.C.E.

Incarnation: The doctrine that Christ, the divine Word, assumed human nature. (How to say this was much disputed during the fourth and fifth centuries.)

Jerome (Hieronymus, Girolamo, Geronimo): Scholar and ascetic, supervisor of the Vulgate translation of the Bible, and an ally of Augustine during the Pelagian controversy.

Julian of Eclanum: Son of a bishop in southern Italy and friend of influential churchmen, who after 418 led the struggle against the condemnation of Pelagianism. He is usually depicted as either an arch-heretic or a hero of independent inquiry.

Manichaeism: A movement, originating in Mesopotamia, that thought in terms of an ultimate dualism, explaining the world as the result of a conflict between good and evil substances.

Nicenes: The party during the fourth century, named from the Council of Nicaea (325), that opposed Arianism and asserted that the Son is "of the same essence" as the Father.

Old Latin Version: The earliest Latin translation of the Bible, based on the Septuagint, made during the third century and used by Augustine.

Origen (ca. 185–ca. 254): A major theologian and biblical commentator who taught that all souls were created equal, fell through their own choice, and are led back to God through a succession of worlds.

Original sin: The doctrine that the sin of Adam and Eve affects all their descendants with death, desire, and guilt.

Pelagius: A Christian reformer in Rome, born in Britain, who asserted that human beings are always free to obey God, since sinful acts cannot affect human nature.

Philo (ca. 20 B.C.E.–ca. 50 C.E.): A Jewish philosopher in Alexandria who interpreted the Bible along Platonist lines, bringing the Bible and Greek culture closer together.

Predestination: The doctrine that salvation is based on God's choice or "election," not on any prior human response to God's call.

Rufinus the Syrian: A member of Jerome's monastery in Bethlehem, reviser of the New Testament in the Vulgate, and champion of the view that death was not caused by the sin of Adam and Eve.

Septuagint: The Greek translation of the Bible, including the Apocrypha, made in Alexandria between ca. 250 B.C.E. and ca. 100 B.C.E. It was named from the legend that seventy-two translators worked for seventy-two days at the direction of the Egyptian ruler.

Timaeus: Plato's dialogue on the formation of the cosmos, written ca. 360 B.C.E., widely read by Christians and others in the ancient world.

Trinity: The doctrine that God is both one and three. The resolution that developed during the fourth century was that God is one essence in three persons.

Vandals: A Germanic group that crossed the Rhine, settled south of the Danube, then migrated to Gaul (406), Spain (409), and Africa (429).

Vulgate: The Latin translation of the Bible (ca. 380–ca. 400), consisting of Jerome's translation of the Old Testament books directly from the Hebrew and a revision of the Old Latin translation of the New Testament.

NOTES

Introduction

1. L. P. Hartley, *The Go-Between* (London: H. Hamilton, 1953), 9.
2. Augustine, *An Essay on the Development of Christian Doctrine*, I,i,7.

1. Augustine's Journey

1. James J. O'Donnell, *Confessions: Introduction, Text, and Commentary* (Oxford: Oxford University Press, 1992), 1:li-lvi. The most extensive narrative is in Augustine's *On the Happy Life*, i,4-6; there is a shorter but more passionate narrative in *On the Academics*, II,ii,5.
2. Augustine, *Confessions*, I,i,1. (All quotations from *The Confessions* are the author's translation.)
3. Ibid., III,iii,5.
4. Augustine, *Sermon Dolbeau*, 2,5.
5. Augustine, *Confessions*, IV,iv,7-viii,13.
6. Ibid., VI,xv,25.
7. Augustine, *On the Happy Life*, i,1-4.
8. Even in his earliest writings it is clear that Augustine knew that Platonist philosophy was insufficient, that reason must be supplemented by authority, and that one must be "drawn" by God, inwardly as well as outwardly. The famous prayer, "If you give what you command, command what you will" (*Confessions*, X,xxix,40; xxxi,45; xxxvii,60), is anticipated as early as the *Soliloquies* (I,i,5) and continues to be stated throughout his life. See Pierre-Marie Hombert, *Gloria Gratiae. Se glorifier en Dieu, principe et fin de la théologie augustinienne de la grâce* (Paris: Institut d'Études Augustiniennes, 1996), 593-94.
9. F. B. A. Asiedu, "Following the Example of a Woman: Augustine's Conversion to Christianity in 386," *Vigiliae Christianae* 57 (2003): 276-306.
10. Augustine, *Confessions*, VIII,ix,21.
11. James J. O'Donnell, *Augustine: Confessions* (Oxford: Clarendon Press, 1992), 1:xlii-xliii; *Augustine: A New Biography* (New York: HarperCollins, 2005), 140-42.
12. Augustine, *Sermon Dolbeau*, 26,15.
13. *Sermon*, 340,1, quoted in *Lumen Gentium*, ch. 4 n. 32.
14. Augustine habitually added "in God" to the statement that all the believers were "one soul and one heart" (Acts 4:32). See George Lawless, *Augustine of Hippo and His Monastic Rule* (Oxford: Clarendon Press, 1987), 133. For a comprehensive survey see Raymond Canning, "Common Good," in *Augustine through the Ages: An Encyclopedia* (ed. Allan D. Fitzgerald; Grand Rapids: Eerdmans, 1999), 219-22.
15. Specific discussions are Augustine's *On Lying* (395) and *Against Lying* (420).

2. Reason's Quest: Augustine the Platonist

1. Augustine, *On True Religion*, iv,6-7.
2. Edward Gibbon, *The Decline and Fall of the Roman Empire* (New York: Modern Library, 1932), 1:448.

3. While Cicero's work is lost, this passage is quoted by Augustine in *On the Trinity*, XIII,v,8.

4. Anders Nygren, *Agape and Eros* (trans. Philip Watson; Philadelphia: Westminster Press, 1953).

5. John Burnaby, *Amor Dei: A Study of the Religion of St. Augustine* (London: Hodder and Stoughton, 1938), 92-100, 117-26, 255-57.

6. Charles W. Kegley, *The Philosophy and Theology of Anders Nygren* (Carbondale: Southern Illinois University Press, 1970), see especially the critiques by John Burnaby (174-86) and Rudolf Johannesson (190-96), as well as Nygren's unrepentant reply (358-65).

7. This is the vision evoked in Plotinus's *Enneads*, I,6 ("On Beauty"), which Augustine certainly read. Other treatises important to him were III,2-3 ("On Providence"), IV,3-4 ("On the Soul"), V,1 ("On the Three Divine Hypostases"), V,5 ("That Intelligibles Are Not Outside Intelligence"), and VI,4-5 ("How That Which Is One and the Same Can Be Everywhere").

8. Augustine, *Confessions*, VII,x,16. (All quotations from *The Confessions* are the author's translation.)

9. Ibid., VII,xx,26.

10. Augustine, *Soliloquies*, II,vi,10; *On True Religion*, xxix,43; *On the Trinity*, XV,xii,21.

11. Augustine, respectively, *On the Academics*, I,iii,7-iv,12; *On Free Choice*, II,ix,26-27; *On the Trinity*, X,x,14; and *City of God*, XXI,15.

12. It is stated partially in *On True Religion*, xxxix,73, but most fully in *City of God*, XI,26. See also *On the Trinity*, X,x,14 and XV,xii,21.

13. Plotinus, *Enneads*, I,6,9; V,1,1. Augustine's most extended discussion of this theme of the soul's eye, its looking, and its seeing is in *Soliloquies*, I,vi,12-vii,14.

14. Augustine, *Confessions*, X,xxvii,38.

15. Ibid., III,vi,11.

16. Plotinus, *Enneads*, VI,4-5, title and discussion.

17. Ibid., V,i,3 and 6.

18. Augustine, *On the Morals of the Catholic Church*, I,xi,18; xii,21; *Exposition of Romans*, 58,8-9.

19. Augustine, *On Free Choice*, II,xi,30-32.

20. Ibid., xii,34; *On True Religion*, xxi,57-58, which is later mentioned in *Epistle*, 162,2.

21. Michel Foucault, *Discipline and Punish: The Birth of the Prison* (New York: Vintage Books, 1979), 187, 202.

22. Augustine, *Confessions*, III,vi,10-viii,16.

23. The similarities are traced at length by J. Joyce Schuld, *Foucault and Augustine: Reconsidering Power and Love* (Notre Dame: University of Notre Dame Press, 2003).

3. Why Evil? Answering the Manichaeans

1. Augustine, *Confessions*, VII,ii,3.

2. René Girard, *Violence and the Sacred* (trans. Patrick Gregory; Baltimore: Johns Hopkins University Press, 1977), passim; *The Scapegoat* (trans. Yvonne Freccero; Baltimore: Johns Hopkins University Press, 1986).

3. Augustine, *Enchiridion*, iii,11; cf. xxiv,96 and xxvi,100.

4. Augustine, *On Genesis against the Manichees*, I,xvi,25-26.

5. Augustine, *Confessions*, I,xiii,21.

6. Ibid., III,ii,2.

7. Augustine, *On Free Choice*, II,xx,54; *City of God*, XII,7.

8. Author's adaptation of Augustine, *City of God*, III,14.

9. Author's adaptation of Augustine, *Against Faustus*, XXII,74.

10. Hannah Arendt, *Eichmann in Jerusalem: A Report on the Banality of Evil* (New York: Viking Press, 1963).

11. The classic discussion is W. G. Runciman, *Relative Deprivation and Social Justice* (Harmondsworth, U.K.: Penguin Books, 1972), 10-35.

4. Time and Creation: Interpreting Genesis

1. After early starts in *On Genesis against the Manichees* and the *Unfinished Commentary on Genesis*, the major discussions are in the *Confessions* (Books XI–XIII), the *Literal Commentary on Genesis* (twelve books), and *The City of God* (books XI–XIV).

2. Augustine, *Confessions*, XI,xiv,17. (All quotations from *The Confessions* are the author's translation.)

3. Augustine, *City of God*, XVI,9.

4. Ibid., XII,11.

5. Augustine, *Confessions*, XI,xxix,39–xxx,40.

6. Ibid., IX,x,23-26.

7. Preface to "God's Determinations," in *The Poetical Works of Edward Taylor* (ed. Thomas H. Johnson; Princeton: Princeton University Press, 1943), 31.

8. Ibid., XIII,iii,4. This double generosity is anticipated in Plato's *Timaeus*, 41A-B, where the Demiurge or Artisan, having already formed the lesser deities, promises to make them indissoluble despite their intrinsic instability.

9. Augustine, *On the Happy Life*, 1,1; *On Free Choice*, III,xxi, 62; *Epistles*, 166,7.

10. Augustine, *On Free Choice*, III,xi,32–xii,35.

11. Ibid., III,xxiv,71-73.

12. Augustine, *City of God*, XI,13-14; XII,9.

13. Augustine, *Against Julian*, III,154 and 187.

14. John Hick, *Evil and the God of Love* (2nd ed.; New York: Harper & Row, 1977), 295n1.

5. Original Sin and Predestination: Threats to Freedom?

1. For a comprehensive outline of this earliest phase, see Theodore de Bruyne, *Pelagius's Commentary on St Paul's Epistle to the Romans* (Oxford: Clarendon Press, 1993), 1-35. The wider context is laid out in Elizabeth A. Clark, *The Origenist Controversy: The Cultural Construction of an Early Christian Debate* (Princeton: Princeton University Press, 1992).

2. Otto Wermelinger, *Rom und Pelagius. Die theologische Position der römischen Bischöfe im pelagianischen Streit in den Jahren 411-432* (Stuttgart: Anton Hiersemann, 1975), 82-87, 357, 366-68.

3. Augustine, *Confessions*, X,xxix,40-xxxvii,62. (All quotations from *The Confessions* are the author's translation.)

4. The word used in the original Greek, and in the Latin translations, is ambiguous. It could mean "continent." But, the more likely meaning is to "possess and enjoy" personified Wisdom, the subject of this passage. Either way, of course, it is God's gift. Renaissance study of Greek and Latin corrected Augustine's interpretation, starting with the French and English translations published in 1560 in Geneva.

5. Pelagius's *Letter to Demetrias*, 8,3. For a clear, logical analysis of the rival positions, see Marianne Djuth, "Possibility," in *Augustine through the Ages: An Encyclopedia* (Grand Rapids: Eerdmans, 1999), 663-67.

6. Augustine, *Sermon*, 131,10.
7. Jane E. Merdinger, *Rome and the African Church in the Time of Augustine* (New Haven: Yale University Press, 1997), 190, 206.
8. Augustine's *Epistles*, 194.
9. This is stated most clearly in *Reconsiderations*, I,15,2-3.
10. *On the Predestination of Saints*, iv,8.
11. This has been suggested by Pierre-Marie Hombert, *Gloria Gratiae. Se glorifier en Dieu, principe et fin de la théologie augustinienne de la grâce* (Paris: Institut d'Études Augustiniennes, 1996), 112-14.
12. This motif is still the subject of learned argument, much of it showing how the original Stoic theory was misunderstood, adapted, or corrected by others in antiquity. See especially Richard Sorabji, *Emotion and Peace of Mind: From Stoic Agitation to Christian Temptation* (Gifford Lectures; Oxford: Oxford University Press, 2000), who sees misunderstandings where others see imaginative adaptations.
13. Augustine, *On the Merits and Remission of Sins*, II,xix,32; *Against Two Letters of the Pelagians*, I,xii,27; *Enchiridion*, xxii,81 and xxxi,118; *On Continence*, 20; and the *Unfinished Work against Julian*, I,107; II,217; and II,226.
14. Augustine, *On Rebuke and Grace*, xiv,45.
15. Marvin N. Olasky, *The Tragedy of American Compassion* (Washington, D.C.: Regnery Gateway, 1992), 10-11, 80-98, 116-33, 217-33.
16. William Sloane Coffin, *Credo* (Louisville: Westminster John Knox Press, 2004), 6, 147, 172.

6. The Church and the Sacraments: Unity in Grace across Space and Time

1. Augustine, *On Baptism*, II,vi,8.
2. See J. Patout Burns, "Appropriating Augustine Appropriating Cyprian," *Augustinian Studies* 36 (2005): 1-16, esp. 12-15.
3. Maureen A. Tilley, *The Bible in Christian North Africa: The Donatist World* (Minneapolis: Fortress Press, 1997), 104-12, 170.
4. Augustine, *On Christian Instruction*, III,xxxii,45.
5. For a summary and references to recent scholarship, see Paula Fredriksen, "Tyconius," in *Augustine through the Ages: An Encyclopedia* (Grand Rapids: Eerdmans, 1999), 853-55.
6. Augustine, *Sermons on John*, 26 (paragraphs 12, 15, 18).
7. Author's adaptation of Augustine, *Sermons on John*, 80,3.
8. Cf. *Sermons on John*, 50,4.
9. Augustine, *Sermons on the Letter of John*, vii,8; x,7.
10. Augustine, *On Instructing Beginners*, iii,6; xix,33.

7. Trinity and Incarnation: Shaping Doctrine in the West

1. Augustine, *On the Lord's Sermon on the Mount*, I,xxii,75; *Unfinished Exposition of Romans*, 11-13; *Sermon 71*.
2. Augustine, *On the First Epistle of John*, vii,6; *On the Trinity*, VIII,vii,10–x,12.
3. Augustine himself suggests this in the *Sermons on the First Epistle of John*, viii,12-14.
4. Cf. Augustine, *On the Trinity*, V,viii,9 and VIII,i,1.
5. Augustine, *Confessions*, VII,xix,25. (All quotations from *The Confessions* are the author's translation.)

6. Both the metaphor of mixture and the expression "unity of person" appear for the first time in *Epistle* 137, written about 411–412; it is not clear what Augustine's immediate source was.

7. Augustine, *Enchiridion*, xii,20; *On the Predestination of the Saints*, xv,30-31; *On the Gift of Perseverance*, xxiv,67.

8. Augustine, *Against the Sermon of the Arians*, 8.

9. Augustine, *Sermon*, 240,5; *City of God*, IX,15 and X,29. Plato's discussion is in *Timaeus*, 31B-32B, 36A-B.

10. Edward Caswall, *Hymns and Poems* (2nd ed.; London: Burns, Oates, and Co., 1873), 152.

11. The classic discussion is Augustine's *City of God*, X,4-6.

12. Augustine, *Confessions*, IX,xiii,36.

13. René Girard, *Things Hidden Since the Foundation of the World* (trans. Stephen Bann and Michael Metteer; Stanford: Stanford University Press, 1987).

8. Citizens and Sojourners: Living in Two Cities

1. From his correspondence it appears that Books I–III were written in 412–413; IV–V by 415; VI–X in 416; XI–XIV in 417–418; XV–XVII in 419; XVIII in 420–425; and XIX–XXII in 425–427.

2. See Philip Jenkins, *The Next Christendom: The Coming of Global Christianity* (Oxford: Oxford University Press, 2002). A contrasting perspective, trying to understand and account for the widespread distrust of the West, is Ian Burima and Avishai Margalit, *Occidentalism: The West in the Eyes of Its Enemies* (New York: Penguin, 2004).

3. Augustine, *City of God*, XI,7; cf. Augustine, *Confessions*, XII,xv,21; XIII,xv,18.

4. Augustine, *On Christian Instruction*, II,xxiii,35–xxiv,37; III,vii,11–ix,13.

5. Augustine, *City of God*, II,20.

6. Augustine, *On Free Choice*, I,xv,32.

7. Augustine, *Sermons on John*, 77,4.

8. Augustine, *Epistles*, 93,iii,9, written about 408.

9. Ibid., 93,ii,8, written 407–408; my translation.

10. Augustine, *Epistles*, 173,2-3, written about 412–414 to a Donatist.

11. The rambling discussion spanning *City of God*, XIX,17-26, can be characterized in all of these ways and more. For those who like close analysis and deconstruction, this passage is a prime candidate.

12. James Davison Hunter, *Culture Wars: The Struggle to Define America* (New York: Basic Books, 1991), 107-32.

13. James Davison Hunter, *Before the Shooting Begins: Searching for Democracy in America's Culture War* (New York: Basic Books, 1994), 215-26.

14. This line of analysis is articulated concisely by Ellen Willis, "Freedom from Religion: What's at Stake in Faith-Based Politics," *The Nation* (February 19, 2001): 11-16.

9. The Sunset Years: Creating a Heritage

1. See Jane E. Merdinger, *Rome and the African Church in the Time of Augustine* (New Haven: Yale University Press, 1997), 148-52.

2. John Burnaby, *Amor Dei: A Study of the Religion of St. Augustine* (London: Hodder and Stoughton, 1938), 231.

3. Augustine, *On the Gift of Perseverance*, xxii,57-62.

4. Augustine, *On the Predestination of Saints*, xi,21.

5. Augustine, *City of God*, XX,8-9; also XXI,15-16. This is another point that Augustine picked up from Tyconius, the renegade Donatist.

6. There is a parallel discussion in *On Faith in Things Not Seen*, written about the same time.

7. Augustine, *City of God*, XXII,5-7.

8. James J. O'Donnell, *Augustine: A New Biography* (New York: HarperCollins, 2005), 311, 318-19.

10. Footnotes, Queries, and Obituaries to Augustine

1. Augustine, *On Marriage and Concupiscence*, II,iii,9; *Against Two Letters of the Pelagians*, III,ix,25.

2. Friedrich Schleiermacher, *The Christian Faith*, §22,2; §80,4.

3. This has been argued by Carol Harrison, "'The Most Intimate Feeling of My Mind': The Permanence of Grace in Augustine's Early Theological Practice," *Augustinian Studies* 36 (2005): 51-58.

4. Augustine, *City of God*, X,30.

SELECTED BIBLIOGRAPHY

Note: All listings are in chronological order of publication.

Augustine's works are so numerous that anyone who claims to have read all of them is lying. That is what Possidius implied soon after Augustine's death, and it was said explicitly by Isidore of Seville two centuries later. Augustine's works were widely copied throughout the Middle Ages, and printed editions began to be produced during the Renaissance. The chief "critical editions" of the Latin text are in the following series:

Patrologia latina. Edited by J.-P. Migne. 217 vols. Paris, 1844-1864.

Corpus scriptorum ecclesiasticorum latinorum. Vienna: [various publishers], 1865–

Sources chrétiennes. Paris: Cerf, 1941–.

Oeuvres de Saint Augustin. Bibliothèque augustinienne. Paris: Desclée de Brouwer, 1949–.

Corpus Christianorum: Series latina. Turnhout: 1953–.

New discoveries are still made. Previously unknown letters were identified by Johannes Divjak in 1975, and previously unknown sermons by François Dolbeau in 1990. These have now been edited and translated.

There is a standard method of citing Augustine's works: book (when there are multiple books in a work), chapter, and paragraph. Paragraph numbers usually increase faster than chapter numbers, but they run in parallel. In this book, lower-case Roman numerals are used for chapters, and Arabic numerals for paragraphs.

Translations

There are several series of translations of selected works into English:

The Nicene and Post-Nicene Fathers, Series 1. Edited by Philip Schaff. 1886–1889. Repr. Peabody, Mass.: Hendrickson, 1994.

Ancient Christian Writers. Westminster, Md.: Newman Press, 1946–.

Fathers of the Church. New York: Fathers of the Church; Washington, D.C.: Catholic University of America Press, 1947–.

The most recent, still in process but intended to become the most complete, is

The Works of Saint Augustine: A Translation for the 21st Century. Brooklyn: New City Press, 1990–.

Reference Tools

Augustinus-Lexikon [articles in English, French, and German]. Basel: Schwabe, 1986–.

Thesaurus Augustinianus [microfiche concordance of the Latin words in Augustine's writings]. Turnhout: Brepols, 1989.

Augustine through the Ages: An Encyclopedia. Grand Rapids: Eerdmans, 1999. [Works are listed on pp. xxxv-il.]

Chronology

La Bonnardière, Anne Marie. *Biblia Augustiniana.* Paris: Études Augustiniennes, 1960–1975.

———. *Recherches de chronologie augustinienne.* Paris: Études Augustiniennes, 1965.

Perler, Othmar. *Les voyages de saint Augustin.* Paris: Études Augustiniennes, 1969.

Hombert, Pierre-Marie. *Nouvelles recherches de chronologie augustinienne.* Paris: Institut d'Études Augustiniennes, 2000.

General and Biographical Studies

Burnaby, John. *Amor Dei: A Study of the Religion of St. Augustine.* London: Hodder & Stoughton, 1938.

Courcelle, Pierre. *Recherches sur les Confessions de saint Augustin.* Paris: Boccard, 1950. Second edition, 1968.

Gilson, Etienne. *The Christian Philosophy of St. Augustine.* New York: Random House, 1960.

Van der Meer, Fredrik. *Augustine the Bishop: Religion and Society at the Dawn of the Middle Ages.* Translated by Brian Battershaw and G. R. Lamb. London: Sheed & Ward, 1961.

Bonner, Gerald. *St. Augustine of Hippo: Life and Controversies*. Philadelphia: Westminster, 1963. Third edition, Norwich: Canterbury, 2002.

Brown, Peter. *Augustine of Hippo: A Biography*. Berkeley: University of California Press, 1967. New edition 2000.

TeSelle, Eugene. *Augustine the Theologian*. New York: Herder and Herder, 1970. Repr., Eugene, Ore.: Wipf and Stock, 2002.

O'Connell, Robert J. *The Origin of the Soul in St. Augustine's Later Works*. New York: Fordham University Press, 1987.

O'Daly, Gerard. *Augustine's Philosophy of Mind*. Berkeley: University of California Press, 1987.

O'Donnell, James J. *Confessions: Introduction and Text*. 3 vols. Oxford: Clarendon Press, 1992.

Rist, J. M. *Augustine: Ancient Thought Baptized*. Cambridge: Cambridge University Press, 1994.

Dodaro, Robert, and George Lawless. *Augustine and His Critics: Essays in Honour of Gerald Bonner*. London: Routledge, 2000.

Harrison, Carol. *Augustine: Christian Truth and Fractured Humanity*. Christian Theology in Context. Oxford: Oxford University Press, 2000.

Lancel, Serge. *Saint Augustine*. Translated by Antonia Nevill. London: SCM Press, 2002.

O'Donnell, James J. *Augustine: A New Biography*. New York: Ecco, 2005.

Monasticism

Lawless, George. *Augustine of Hippo and His Monastic Rule*. Oxford: Clarendon Press, 1987.

Mysticism and Spirituality

Clark, Mary T., trans. *Augustine of Hippo: Selected Writings*. Classics of Western Spirituality. Mahwah, N.J.: Paulist Press, 1984.

Augustine and Women

Børresen, Kari Elisabeth. *Subordination and Equivalence: The Nature and Role of Women in Augustine and Thomas Aquinas*. Translated by Charles H. Talbot. Washington: University Press of America, 1981.

Clark, Elizabeth A. *Ascetic Piety and Women's Faith: Essays on Late Ancient Christianity.* Lewisdon, N.Y.: Edwin Mellen Press, 1986.

Miles, Margaret. *Desire and Delight: A New Reading of Augustine's "Confessions."* New York: Crossroad, 1992.

Power, Kim. *Veiled Desire: Augustine on Women.* New York: Continuum, 1996.

The Church in Africa

Willis, G. G. *Saint Augustine and the Donatist Controversy.* London: S.P.C.K., 1950.

Frend, W. H. C. *The Donatist Church: A Movement of Protest in Roman North Africa.* Oxford: Clarendon Press, 1952.

Merdinger, Jane E. *Rome and the African Church in the Time of Augustine.* New Haven: Yale University Press, 1997.

Tilley, Maureen. *The Bible in Christian North Africa: The Donatist World.* Minneapolis: Fortress Press, 1997.

Lepelley, Claude. *Aspects de l'Afrique romaine: les cités, la vie rurale, le Christianisme.* Bari, Italy: Edipuglia, 2001.

Burns, J. Patout. *Cyprian the Bishop.* London: Routledge, 2002.

The Pelagian Controversy

Evans, Robert F. *Pelagius: Inquiries and Reappraisals.* New York: Seabury Press, 1968.

Wermelinger, Otto. *Rom und Pelagius. Die theologische Position der römischen Bischöfe im pelagianischen Streit in den Jahren 411–432.* Päpste und Papsttum 7. Stuttgart: Anton Hiersemann, 1975.

Rees, B. R. *Pelagius: A Reluctant Heretic.* Woodbridge: Boydell Press, 1988.

Clark, Elizabeth A. *The Origenist Controversy: The Cultural Construction of an Early Christian Debate.* Princeton: Princeton University Press, 1992.

Wetzel, James. *Augustine and the Limits of Virtue.* Cambridge: Cambridge University Press, 1992.

De Bruyn, Theodore, trans. *Pelagius's Commentary on St Paul's Epistle to the Romans.* Oxford Early Christian Studies. Oxford: Clarendon Press, 1993.

Lössl, Josef. *Julian von Aeclanum: Studien zu seinem Leben, seinem Werk, seiner Lehre und ihrer Überlieferung.* Leiden: Brill, 2001.

Political Thought

Combès, Gustave. *La doctrine politique de saint Augustin.* Paris: Plon, 1927.

Deane, Herbert A. *The Political and Social Ideas of St. Augustine.* New York: Columbia University Press, 1963.

Markus, R. A. *Saeculum: History and Society in the Theology of St. Augustine.* Cambridge: Cambridge University Press, 1970.

Van Oort, Johannes. *Jerusalem and Babylon: A Study into Augustine's City of God and the Sources of His Doctrine of the Two Cities.* Leiden: E. J. Brill, 1991.

TeSelle, Eugene. *Living in Two Cities: Augustinian Trajectories in Political Thought.* Scranton: Scranton University Press, 1998.

Critical Perspectives on Augustine

Nygren, Anders. *Agape and Eros.* Translated by Philip Watson. Philadelphia: Westminster Press, 1952.

Hick, John. *Evil and the God of Love.* Rev. ed. New York: Harper & Row, 1977.

Ricoeur, Paul. *The Symbolism of Evil.* New York: Harper & Row, 1967.

Pagels, Elaine. *Adam, Eve, and the Serpent.* New York: Vintage, 1988.

Capps, Donald, and James E. Dittes, eds. *The Hunger of the Heart: Reflections on the Confessions of Augustine.* Monograph Series 8. West Lafayette, Ind.: Society for the Scientific Study of Religion, 1990.

Flasch, Kurt. *Logik des Schreckens.* 2d ed. Mainz, Germany: Dieterich, 1995.

Connolly, William F. *The Augustinian Imperative: A Reflection on the Politics of Morality.* Newbury Park, Calif.: Sage Publications, 1993.

Lyotard, Jean-François. *The Confession of Augustine.* Translated by Richard Beardsworth. Stanford: Stanford University Press, 2000.

Schuld, J. Joyce. *Foucault and Augustine: Reconsidering Power and Love.* Notre Dame: University of Notre Dame Press, 2003.

SCRIPTURE INDEX

CITATIONS FROM AUGUSTINE'S WORKS

CITATIONS FROM OTHER ANCIENT AUTHORS

CITATIONS FROM MODERN AUTHORS

Index of Topics, Places, and Persons